To Diane —

All best wishes

To a great baseball

fan —

Your pal,

Maury Allen

China Spy

Maury Allen

Gazette Press, Inc.
16 School Street
Yonkers, New York 10701

Published by

Gazette Press
16 School Street
Yonkers, New York 10701

First edition
ISBN: 0-9663322-0-2

Published in the United States of America

Library of Congress Catalog Number: 97-95325

Contents

Dedicated to the memory of

Hugh Francis Redmond

who gave his life in the service of his country

Chapter 1

A Neighborhood Pal

The grave is on a knoll above a small foot path in the middle of the one hundred year old Oakland Cemetery in Yonkers, New York. Some headstones in the thirty five acre field are bent with time. On a sunny day, birch trees provide pleasant shade. There are three headstones in this one, unobtrusive plot. A small American flag is set deeply in the soft dirt in front of the middle stone.

There is a slight glistening on this one center stone, as if it had been scrubbed and cleaned a little more often than any others. It sits higher than the other two, the dirt below a little smoother, a large yellow flower stuck awkwardly in its midst. Some yards away workmen in coveralls dig another grave in the earth, the digging and falling dirt from their shovels making the only discernible sounds on this quiet spring afternoon. Sounds from cars passing outside the cemetery gates on Saw Mill River Road seem very distant. The names are chiseled into the stone. The center stone reads:

REDMOND
Hugh Francis
1919 — 1970
His Country Above All Else
In God's Loving Care

The stone to the left is that of the father, Hugh Francis Redmond — 1884 — 1959 and to the right is that of the mother, Ruth Redmond — 1897 — 1973.

The caretaker seemed unwilling to discuss what he knew of the burial of Hugh Francis Redmond, of what the funeral was like, of who had planted the flag or the flower, of where the bills for upkeep were directed.

"It's perpetual care," he says, as he leans on the wall of his small office, his hand on the phone, his eyes fixed outside the window as if expecting some uninvited guest. "The funeral parlor, Flynn's, they made the arrangements. I think I was off that day. That's right — vacation time, wasn't it? Let's see, that was August 1970, wasn't it?" He opened a large book, ran his fingers down a page, found what he was looking for. "Yep, here it is, August 3, 1970, Hugh Francis Redmond, that's all I can tell you. I gotta get to work now. Lots to do." He closes the book, moves toward the office door and walks out to his small car. He opens the car door and turns back quickly toward his office.

"Redmond? Yeah, I guess everybody knows he was a CIA fellow now, don't they?"

Oakland Cemetery is located on a busy, industrial street in Yonkers, the fourth largest city in New York State, across from a wire factory and a bakery products company. The city population has grown to nearly two hundred thousand. Located some ten miles north of Manhattan, Yonkers once flourished as a summer residential area for New York bankers and industrialists. With easy access to Hudson River transportation and New York City, factories soon located there and the character of the city changed for the worse shortly after World War I. By the early 1930s it was a city of light industry, wooden factories, small shops with blue collar workers, Italians, Irish and Eastern Europeans. The rich had moved north and east to less densely populated parts of Westchester County.

About the only attraction Yonkers has for people from New York City now is Yonkers Raceway, a sprawling harness track located on the east side of town off one of the main thoroughfares, Yonkers Avenue, and hard by the south end of the Governor Thomas E. Dewey Thruway. The track operates from early spring to early winter, the lights of the track lighting up the nearby sky, the noise coming in rushes across the soft, summer nights when the parking lots are crowded and the stands are filled.

A few doors south of the intersection of Yonkers and Central Park Avenue, past a small boutique, past a small dress shop is Johnny Bauer's Paradise Bar. It is a balmy night in early spring. The lights from the track glow and form shadows across most of the street. There are a few posters in the window of the Paradise, a faded Roosevelt High School basketball schedule and an advertisement for Schaefer beer. A large poster on the door reads ***BRING OUR POWs HOME.***

There is the usual collection of Friday night fans in a friendly neighborhood bar, two pretty girls in their early twenties talking quietly at one end, a middle aged man a couple of seats away staring at a basketball game on the television set, two young men dressed in work clothes talking with the bartender, and an older man, dreamy eyed, staring with a blank expression at the corner juke box.

"Do you know Bernie Connolly?"

"Right there," said the bartender, "the guy with the red jacket."

Connolly is seventy one years old — a husky, handsome man with a round face and large ears. He is athletic looking, with a strong facial resemblance to an old New York basketball player named Dick McGuire.

"Yeah, I'm Connolly," he says, pushing out a large hand. What'll you have?"

"A beer is fine."

The meeting had been set earlier. Connolly said he would be happy to talk about Hugh Redmond. He suggested Johnny's Paradise Bar because he used to live a couple of blocks away on Lorimer Street and Hugh Redmond lived around the corner on Belmont Avenue.

"I was about ten or eleven when I first met Hughie. He was three or four years older than me, but we hung out together — a whole crowd of us — maybe ten, fifteen guys. Bobby Sackett will be in soon, he's closer in age to Hughie. After the war Hughie and I were together a lot. We both had been through the war, combat and all that makes everybody older. It didn't matter how old I was then, I still looked up to Hughie."

Connolly pulled out a cigarette and lit it. He dropped the pack on the bar. "We used to hang out on the street, across Yonkers Avenue there, in

Bebe's pool room. Hughie was good at pool. He would go in there, somebody would challenge him to a game. He wouldn't say much, just take off his coat and start playing. He was a damn good pool shooter. Damn, Redmond was good at everything he done. Sure I looked up to him. He had been around, he was a little older — he was a hero to me."

Connolly worked in a Post Office, retiring after more than a quarter of a century of service.

"I remember when Redmond died and the Chinese shipped his body back here. They held the funeral at Flynn's and I told my supervisor I was taking the day off. He asked me why and I told him I was going to Hugh Redmond's funeral. He asked me, 'Did you know him?' I never told nobody outside the neighborhood. I didn't talk about Hugh all those years he was held by the Communists. I wrote him a couple of letters, I called his mother once. I never heard from him, from anybody. I always thought he'd get out. He was a tough guy, strong, as hard as nails. I figured if anybody could survive in a Chinese prison it would be Hughie Redmond. I never let on what I knew. All those stories about Redmond working for an American import-export firm. People in town knew what he did. Hell, I was there the day he got his assignment to report to the CIA for overseas duty."

Connolly pulled another cigarette from his pack. He ordered two more beers. He rubbed his hand through his hair and his face suddenly seemed tired and older.

"I hope this doesn't hurt Hughie and his family," he said softly. "What with all this stuff going on nowadays about the CIA, I wouldn't want to hurt him. I'd like to help him, help his memory I mean. I think Hugh Redmond was a hero — a legitimate hero, a guy we could all respect. I mean, this town and the people around here. He was a hero in the war, a paratrooper, a guy who made all the big jumps, then went into the CIA and held out against the Chinese. I think he should get a medal."

The bartender brought the beers. Connolly continued to talk. He looked straight ahead, staring at a picture of Babe Ruth that hung over the bar.

"We worked together, me, Hughie and Tommy Mulligan, in this

Jewish camp in the Poconos, Camp Tamiment they called it, and we all got jobs as busboys. It was the summer of '46, after we had all gotten back from the war. Redmond had this bad leg wound and he was finally starting to move good. We thought a summer job would be fun. We didn't want the money from the 52-20 club. We worked at the camp for a month and Redmond got this letter from home. It was his orders. I was there when he opened it up. He was ordered to report to the State Department, the OSS I think it was called then, and go on to China."

The door was pushed open now and a hefty man with gray, wavy hair walked to the bar. He slapped Connolly on the back, was introduced to the visitor and waved to the bartender. "A shot and a beer, Johnny," he said.

We were just talking about the time Hughie went away to join the OSS," said Connolly. "Everybody in town knew where he was going, right?"

"Oh sure," said Bobby Sackett. "That's what always made me laugh all those years the committee here in town was trying to get him out. They'd put this stuff in the papers about him being in the import-export business in Shanghai. One day he was working in camp as a busboy and the next day he was a big executive with an import-export firm in China. They gotta be able to come up with better cover stories than that."

Sackett sipped his whiskey and washed the taste away with his beer. He took a peek at the basketball game on television as someone stole a pass and scored on a lay-up.

"Redmond was a little older than me. He was more friendly with my brother Vince and they all hung out down at Shady Field and played ball all day long. Redmond was a good athlete, very good at every sport — baseball, basketball, football and all the kid games. Kick the can, ring-a-levio — anything to do with running. He could run faster than any kid in the neighborhood."

Connolly sipped at his beer and said, "It's been a long time since I thought of Redmond. I remember when we all hung out in the candy store down here — Baker's — and we'd wait for the papers at night to read the sports news. We used to be together in a group — Redmond, Tommy

Ferguson, he got killed in the war, Tom Gomar, he died in the war, too. I bet a dozen guys in our group died in the war. We were all about the same age and I remember the day the war started. We were in Bebe's pool room. It wasn't a question of *if* we would go — it was *when* we would go. If I had a kid draft age now, I don't know if I'd be upset if he went to Canada if we started fighting somebody again. We used to know why we got killed in a war. Now we don't know. When I went away, I prayed I didn't get killed. I didn't care about losing an arm or a leg. I had a brother and he drowned when he was ten and my mother — she used to be pretty and dark haired — got old and her hair turned white overnight. She couldn't have survived if I got killed in the war. Hey, Bobby, who else got killed in the war?"

"Well, there was Tommy Lyons, Dan Fitzgerald, Oscar Birpo...

"Azzinaro...what was his name? ...Johnny Azzinaro...and Carl Martz...Sal Imbrogummo...Kohler, Dick Kohler...and Monagana — what was his first name... we called him Red — I don't remember his real name."

"...and Louis Lavertrandie — good punch ball player."

"Yeah, I think they got a plaque down near the park for all of them. We all knew we'd go. Redmond was worried about his parents because they didn't have any money. He was worried about how they would manage if he went. One of the older guys said he wouldn't go. He said he was married and was going to pull out all his teeth. He heard the Army didn't take guys without teeth."

Sackett watched the basketball game. Then he finished his drink and ordered another round. "We didn't have a lot of money," Sackett said. "But Redmond's family always seemed worse off than anybody else's in the neighborhood. His father was a janitor of the house they lived in on Belmont Avenue and he always walked around the streets with those work clothes on, and big red suspenders. He had a chew of tobacco in his mouth all the time, had no teeth and always walked with his head down. Walked by everybody, never said hello to anyone. He was a strange old man. The mother too, very quiet. They stayed by themselves all the time. We'd go over to Hughie's house and all the parents would be sitting outside on the stoops. Not them. You never saw them on the street except when the old lady was carrying groceries or the old man was walking down to Baker's for a package of chewing tobacco."

Connolly suddenly looked at Sackett and asked, "Do you remember Redmond's sister? It was Ruth, right? She was tough — a real tomboy."

"Yeah," said Sackett, "one time we were all playing on our sleds and some guy knocked her off her sled. She was a little thing then, built like her mother who was small, but she got up, got a snowball, washed that guy's face in the snow and knocked him right off his sled, right on his ass. How is she now — you see her?"

"She's fine, she's a grandmother. Lives upstate. She has a nice home and a nice family."

"We had fun as kids," Connolly said. "No TV, just go out and play. It ain't the same now. We all went off to war and the guys that came back just picked up where we left off. Redmond had seen a lot of action and was hurt bad. But we all had seen action. It was no big deal. He limped when he first got back but he didn't talk much about the war. What the hell was there to talk about? We'd all been there."

Connolly began to smile. He seemed on the verge of telling a story but wasn't sure if he should.

"I'll tell you this but I don't know how it will sound," he said. "Well, anyway, after the war we were in Bebe's and Redmond comes over to me and says, 'Wanna get laid?' This was 1946 now and we'd all been in the war and nothing shocked us but I had to laugh at that. Everybody thought Hughie was a quiet, shy guy. I said sure and we got in his car and drove downtown. 'Where are we going?' I asked him. Hughie said 'Eighty second street.' He drove and we smoked cigarettes and talked about looking for jobs. Then we pulled up in front of this dumpy old building on Eighty second in Manhattan. 'This is it, Bernie. This is my whore house.' We paid a couple of bucks and that was it. Don't let anybody tell you that Hughie Redmond didn't know his way around."

Another round was ordered and Sackett, a man who seems to have a perpetual grin on his face said, "Hugh taught me the facts of life."

Sackett took a sip of his whiskey, a large swallow of beer and told his story. "I was a kid," he said, "maybe thirteen, fourteen at the most and Hugh was sixteen, and we were on a street corner, about four of us near his house on Belmont. We were always talking about sex and how you did it. Nobody really knew, they just made out like they did. 'I know,' Hugh said. Then he runs off to his house and comes back with this book. It had drawings of naked women and parts of the body and everything. He starts explaining how you did it and how you make a baby and what a woman with a baby inside looks like. We're fascinated, of course, but nobody really believes it. The next day a woman walks down the street and she is about nine months pregnant. One of the guys sees her and in a loud voice says, 'Hey, she's pregnant.' His mother is standing right there when he says it and she comes up screaming, 'What did you say, what do you know about that stuff, what have you been doing, you no good bum, ya.' She gives him a good smack across the mouth and sends him inside.

The next day my mother gets a phone call. 'Who's teaching the kids all that dirty garbage about having babies?' My mother just hung up on her."

Sackett said he remembered when Redmond came back from the war. "He was bigger, stronger, he wobbled a little bit," Sackett said. "Redmond wasn't tall — about five feet six inches, maybe a hundred and fifty pounds, but he was built well, like a bull, barrel chested and with his bad leg and the way he walked we took to calling him Jimmy Cagney. Redmond didn't look for fights, it wasn't that, but he was a tough guy. He could handle himself. The other tough guy on the street was Muggsy Falvey. Go find him. He'll tell you some stories about Redmond. They were in the paratroopers together."

The bar was crowded now and the jukebox was being played louder and the smoke was growing thick. Bernie Connolly sipped at his beer and a look of sadness came over his face.

"Why did he die? What for? What good did it do? He was a spy and they caught him. He should have said he was a spy, made up some story, admitted what they wanted him to admit and gone the hell home. That's what all the others did. I followed all those cases in the papers — the fliers that got shot down, the priests, all of them the Chinese captured.

After a while they let them all go. They said they were spies, they admitted it, they promised they wouldn't do it again and they went home. Redmond never admitted anything. He became a cause. What good did it do? Why the hell did he waste his life in a Chinese prison?"

Bobby Sackett was not smiling. "I remember at the funeral," he said, "a few of us from the old days went down there. Mostly it was people from the media and the politicians from town — they took it over. They had his remains in a small casket. They said his body was cremated. They said it was Hugh Redmond. Hell, it could have a pile of leaves in there, who the hell would ever know?"

The clock on the bank at the corner said it was five minutes after one. Most of the lights from the Yonkers racetrack were turned off. A gentle breeze threw some old programs around on Yonkers Avenue.

Chapter 2

Mystery Man

A small statue of a handsome young soldier stands near a fountain in the town of Kilkenny in southern Ireland. The words engraved in the stone are difficult to read. The statue is dedicated to The *Fighting Redmonds*.

Ruth Redmond Boyle, a small, pretty, slightly overweight grandmother, is seventy three years old. She has light blond hair with streaks of gray. She is a gentle woman with a soft voice. She is sitting in the kitchen of her neatly furnished home in Wurtsboro, New York, some ninety miles north of New York City.

"My father used to talk about that statue in his home town a lot," said Hugh Redmond's kid sister. "He was proud of it. He lived up to the family tradition. So did my brother Hugh."

The senior Hugh Francis Redmond was born in that Irish town of Kilkenny in 1884, the fourth son of a local potato farmer. The family eked out a meager existence from the earth and in 1899, just past his fifteenth birthday, the short, sturdy, light haired boy was sent across the Atlantic on a steamer to make a better life in America. He had the address of an uncle pinned to his undershirt, moved with terror through the complications of his arrival at Ellis Island, crossed into Manhattan by ferry, was befriended by an older Irish immigrant and escorted to a train station. He arrived at the Yonkers home of his uncle shortly before dusk on a blistering summer evening. He carried a paper bag. In it was wrapped a sweater, a pair of trousers, a clean shirt and two pair of socks. He had two dimes left in his pocket as he knocked on the door.

In a few days he was settled comfortably in his uncle's house. He slept on a torn couch in the living room, ate better than he ever had before, and ran errands for his uncle, listening carefully to everything he was told and obeying instructions faithfully. The following year he obtained a job as an apprentice weaver in a rug factory. He paid two dollars a week for his room, a meal that was left on the dining room table for him every night when he came home, and a chance at a hot water bath once a week.

Irish immigrants had been coming to America almost since the first ships sailed from England. The massive wave of Irish immigration did not begin until the second half of the nineteenth century but groups of Irish came earlier, formed their own settlements in America, and enjoyed a community life similar to what they had left behind. Such a settlement was established in the small New York town of Saugerties. Shortly after Thomas Jefferson became president of the United States the first member of the Murphy family, Irish immigrants in Saugerties, was born. Hugh Redmond's mother, Ruth Murphy, was born there in 1897.

"Some members of the Murphy family were born here and others kept coming over from Ireland," says Lester Murphy, Ruth's younger brother and uncle of Hugh Redmond. "I know my mother was born in Saugerties and my father was born in Ireland."

Ruth Murphy, who could trace her lineage in Saugerties back some six generations, was one of eleven children. The family moved to Yonkers in 1909. In 1915, Ruth, a small, fragile, thin-faced girl of eighteen, went to work as a helper in the Alexander Smith carpet factory in Yonkers. There she met, fell in love and married the strong, stocky weaver named Hugh Francis Redmond.

They moved into a small apartment on Lane Street in Yonkers. Their first child, also named Hugh Francis Redmond, was born in that apartment on October 30, 1919. A second child, also named Ruth, was born in the same apartment a little more than two years later. There were no other children.

"My father worked hard, came home, ate his dinner and would fall asleep in a living room chair," remembers Ruth Boyle. "I guess you could say he had no hobbies or interests outside of his work. He had a good sense of humor and when he was younger, I remember him sitting us on his knee and telling funny stories. He would always laugh the loudest at his own story."

Money was always tight. When little Hugh started school at six in 1925, his mother went back to work at the rug factory. Friends and relatives cared for little Ruth until her mother came home.

"Then came the trouble," says Ruth Redmond Boyle. "You know, the business about the fighting Redmonds."

One afternoon the foreman of the factory was talking to Ruth Redmond, assigning her some work, suggesting ways she could finish faster. He also began commenting on her appearance, addressing her in a manner that seemed removed from the routine employer to employee relationship.

"My father was working on a machine nearby," says Ruth Boyle. "He didn't ask any questions. He just got up from his machine, walked over to the foreman slowly and knocked him across a table."

Hugh Redmond was fired from his job. Ruth Redmond, making ten dollars a week, was allowed to stay on.

Redmond could not find another job. He had lost his position with the only skill he knew, rug weaving. He sat at home, depressed, waiting for his wife to get home, questioning her carefully about her day, and waiting, hoping to be called back to the factory after Ruth reported an increase in business. No such call ever came.

One afternoon Redmond saw an advertisement in the Yonkers paper. A new apartment house at 19 Intervale Place in south Yonkers was looking for a janitor. A three room apartment would be given free in exchange for the work. Hugh Redmond took the job and the family moved. Ruth continued working at the factory and little Hugh and his sister often stayed at the home of their Uncle Lester. Then came the stock market crash of 1929.

"I don't remember if Ruth lost her job right away," says Lester Murphy, "but things were very bad for them. We weren't what you would call a close family but we agreed to take young Hughie in with us."

Lester Murphy lives in Briarcliff Manor, a pleasant tree-lined suburb north of New York City. He is retired after years as the head custodian in the Yonkers school system.

"I was working for the Otis Elevator Company then, you know — 1929, 1930 — in around there. We lived over on Lockwood Avenue then and the boy used to rush through the door after school, throw his books in his room and rush out to play. We thought we'd have him only a couple of months but it stretched out for a couple of years."

As a boy young Redmond was slight of build with reddish blond hair that would never stay combed. It gave him an unkempt appearance as he ran about.

"He was a wild kid, not bad, just active, you know, always running after the bigger kids, or playing ball. He was always rushing in and out of the house. He didn't seem much interested in his school work," says Uncle Lester, "just in playing ball."

Lester Murphy laughed when he recalled those days more than half a century ago when he provided a home for his nephew.

"We called him The Lion," said Mr. Murphy. "He was an active boy and we couldn't control him none, so that seemed like a good name, The Lion, like the wildest animal in the jungle."

After Hugh Redmond returned home he would see his uncle only occasionally through the years, even though they lived hardly ten minutes apart.

"My sister Ruth, well, she was a quiet person, kept to herself, wouldn't share things. That's the way she was. She was a good person, a hard worker, honest and decent, but close-mouthed, you know."

What about his nephew's career, his experiences in the war as a paratrooper, his work with the CIA, his time in a Chinese prison, and his death?

"I didn't know anything about that," he said. "My sister Ruth just never talked about personal things. She never talked much about anything."

The Depression deepened in the early 1930s and the Redmonds moved to a new home, where the senior Redmond had another job as a janitor, at 65 Belmont Avenue in the Dunwoodie section of Yonkers. It was located just across Central Park Avenue from the Empire Raceway, later to be known as Yonkers Raceway.

"Hughie used to go over to the track during the racing season and help them park cars," said Ruth Boyle. "He could get a quarter or half a dollar for finding a spot. If a guy wouldn't pay he might come out of the track and find a couple of holes in his tires."

"All the kids used to hustle over there," said old pal Bobby Sackett. "We'd make maybe five bucks a day which was pretty good dough back then. There were older kids out there, too. I remember Hughie's father used to be there. He could really hustle those cars. He'd park them all. He probably would wind up with fifteen or twenty bucks on a busy day."

The senior Redmond worked hard as the janitor at the new three story aluminum frame building on Belmont Avenue. Ruth Redmond continued her job at the rug factory. Their new neighborhood was crowded with kids of blue collar workers.

"There were always kids in the street," says Ruth Boyle." "Hughie would be out there every day. There was a big lot across the street from the house. The boys got together one day and built their own running track. They put up a crossbar and Hugh tried pole vaulting. He ripped his pants and my mother really smacked him for it."

There were only three rooms in the new apartment, so Hugh and his sister had to share the only bedroom. It made them both uncomfortable as they were growing up.

"I guess we weren't really close," says Ruth. "He was older and he was lazy around the house. He had his own friends and didn't have much time for me. The only time he liked me was when they needed me as an extra player for their football games in the lot."

The Redmonds were able to afford a large floor model radio and Hugh and his sister would often sit together on Saturdays and listen to broadcasts of the opera.

"Hugh would sit there all afternoon and listen to Milton Cross. He loved the sound of his voice. My tastes ran more to music for jitterbugging," Ruth said.

One rainy afternoon, after the opera broadcast had ended, Ruth turned the radio dial to a new station. Jitterbug music filled the air.

"Hey, Ruthie," said Hugh, "can you teach me to jitterbug?"

"Sure. Stand like this. Put your hands here. Now move this way, now that way. That's it....now swing me around....that's right...a little more swing....oooh."

Hugh Redmond had twisted and turned his sister completely over his head. She landed hard on the floor and hurt her back.

"I think I was in bed for two days. It was a long time before I would dance with him after that," Ruth said.

Each working night of the week Ruth would prepare dinner while her mother finished work and her father tended to chores around the building. Her brother would read.

"He got the books from school, from the local library, anyplace he could — mysteries, adventure stories, a novel — anything he could get his hands on. He would curl up on a chair, put his feet on the arm rest and read. He could read fast, too. He would finish a book and tell me the whole story in a day."

At home young Redmond had one personality and outside of the house showed another. He was very quiet, slightly withdrawn at home, alone with his books and listening to his music, dreaming of a career as an athlete, devouring the sports pages, running outside any chance he got.

With his friends he was outgoing, witty, warm and a good pal.

"He had a bouncy little walk, sort of a strut," remembers boyhood friend Jack White. "He was a very good athlete. He was sure of himself — a cocky kid in sports, really. In fact, we used to call him 'Coxey.'"

White lived around the corner from the Redmonds. He married a neighborhood girl named Catherine Garrett.

"Hughie was a couple of years ahead of me in school," remembers Mrs. White. "He was a quiet boy, loved sports and stayed away from the girls. I think he was the kind of boy who would back off if he felt you were getting too close to him."

Jack White recalls running in track meets with Hugh when they were both still in grade school at School Number Four in Yonkers.

"They had CYO meets around town and Hughie won a lot of medals in those races. He was a sprinter and I was a distance runner. He had great energy. He wasn't a big kid, maybe weighed 110 pounds when he was twelve, thirteen years old."

Redmond and White joined the Catholic Youth Organization together and wound up being recruited for the CYO boxing team.

"One of the other guys in town, Muggsy Falvey, had a big house over on St. John's Avenue. He had a boxing ring put in that house and we used to work out over there. Sometimes I'd beat him and sometimes he'd beat me. But I'll tell you one thing about him. You might punch Hugh in the nose but you'd never get him to back away."

There was something else about young Redmond that seemed to separate him from his contemporaries. He had an air of mystery about him. He seemed to disappear from his play groups every so often.

"You know how it is with kids. Especially in the summer. You'd be out there every day, the same time, six or eight of us — Muggsy Falvey, Charlie Williams, Tommy Walsh — a whole bunch of us and Hughie. One day somebody would say, 'Hey, any of you guys seen Hughie? I ain't seen him for a week.' We never rang each other's doorbells. We didn't want to bother nobody. If any of the kids wanted to play they would come to the lot, that's where everybody was," said White.

After one week's mysterious disappearance, Redmond showed up in the evening just after darkness fell, and joined the kids in the lot. He was about thirteen then.

"Where you been?" asked Jack White.

"Inside," said Redmond. "Studying."

"Studying? What are you studying? There's nothing to study. It's summer vacation."

"I've been studying the constellations."

Redmond then proceeded to entertain and educate his friends on the formation of the stars in the sky, the Big Dipper and the Little Dipper, Ursa Major and Ursa Minor, Boötes and Orion, until his pals would gasp and exclaim, "Jesus Christ, how did you learn all that crap?"

"He was interested in astronomy and he saved up his car parking money to buy a telescope," Ruth Boyle remembers. "He would sit for hours on the porch and look up at the heavens. He never seemed to tire of it."

Redmond had a variety of interests and they would come and go with the wind. But one interest remained constant.

"He wanted to run in the 1936 Olympics. I think that was the only serious, steady interest of his life at the time," says his sister.

Redmond had studied the times of the track stars in the 1932 Olympics in Los Angeles. He could see himself qualifying in 1936 for the Berlin Olympics. Redmond, White, Muggsy Falvey, Tommy Mulligan and Ray Wik worked together to clear most of the stones from the lot across the street from the Belmont Avenue house. They got rakes and smoothed out the dirt. They planted a hurdles bar in the ground. They were able to construct a crossbar for pole vaulting.

"I remember them out there rain or shine," says Mrs. Catherine Lei, who lived at 61 Belmont Avenue for over half a century.

Mrs. Lei, a sprightly gray haired woman, had a son, Anthony. Anthony no longer lives in Yonkers, but he was a friend of Hugh's.

"Hughie was a good boy, very reserved, very quiet, a gentleman, never any trouble in the neighborhood. He wasn't a juvenile delinquent like some of them today. He just liked to play in that lot and he was out there night and day."

Mrs. Lei walked across the street from her comfortable two story home. She pointed at a brick house on the other side of the street.

"That's where the lot began, right about there and went back all the way to the next street. They made a little noise over there but they were good boys," Mrs. Lei said.

She said she had read all the stories about Redmond through the years in the local papers.

"We heard he was with the CIA but nobody would say anything about that to the Redmonds. They kept to themselves. We might sit outside our house on the street in the summertime for some air. They never did. They always sat upstairs on their little porch," she said.

"I would see Mrs. Redmond walking down the street with the gro-

ceries and if Hughie was around he'd come over and help her. He was a
nice fellow. If he saw me coming down the street with my hands full with
groceries he would come and help me, too. He was a fine young man. It's
a shame what happened to him."

Ray Wik is seventy four years old, at one time an agent of the
Federal Bureau of Investigation, later on an insurance broker in Yonkers.
In the 1930s he lived at 59 Clark Street, a few blocks away from the
Redmonds.

"Hughie was a superb athlete. He could run faster than any kid on
the block," Wik said. "I think he was the best in the neighborhood in any
of our games. He could just go from one game to the next and be tops. In
the summer we would roller skate a lot together and in winter we would
go down to Tibbetts Park and ice skate."

Wik remembered something else. "I can hear his voice, even now. It
was deeper, more masculine, more mature than most of us as a kid," he
said. "Somehow he seemed more grown up, more a man of the world."

"Nobody had any money then," said Wik. "I don't think there was a
kid on that street whose father was making seventy five bucks a week.
Somehow Hughie seemed to have it worse than most of us. He had to
hang on to his clothes longer, well after they were torn and patched a few
times."

"When we got new clothes," recalled Ruth Boyle, "it was a major
family event."

Wik also saw this air of mystery, this aloofness, an air of withdraw-
al about Redmond, especially when someone seemed to be getting too
close to him. No one ever visited Hugh in his own house.

"He never talked that much about money or his father being a janitor but you could feel he was embarrassed," Wik said.

There were special days that Wik remembers, memories that last
through the years. Wik remembers a very special day for Hugh Redmond.

"We were playing baseball in the lot across the street. We had just
started a game without our gloves and now somebody said we should get
our gloves and a bat and have a real game instead of just a catch. Hughie
had this beat up old catcher's glove. This one day he ran inside and came

out with a new, beautiful Bill Dickey model catcher's glove. It was really neat. I don't think I ever saw his face light up like that before," Wik said.

Wik said he could not remember the last time he had thought about Hugh Redmond.

"You know, we're all busy with our own lives, our families, making a living. I was pretty close to Hugh. I followed the whole story later on. Coxey was a great kid. the whole thing was a tragedy," Wik said. "That was one hell of a tragedy."

In the fall of 1934 Hugh Francis Redmond, a month short of fifteen years old, a cleft in his chin and with a scrawny one hundred and twenty five pounds on his five foot two inch frame, entered Roosevelt High School.

"We used to walk down Yonkers Avenue or take a bus for a nickel to get there if we were late," says Gustave Segschneider, one time maintenance mechanic for Westchester County. "Maybe eight or ten of us would go to school together. Hughie was with us at the start and at the finish but not in the middle."

The kids would start out for school and suddenly Redmond would veer off, run in the opposite direction and disappear as he crossed Central Park Avenue.

"He'd be gone ten, fifteen minutes maybe, then he would show up, jogging past us as if we were standing still," Segschneider says. One day Segschneider couldn't stand it anymore. He asked Redmond where he was disappearing to each morning.

"Where do you go when you leave us, Coxey?" Segschneider asked.

"Just across the street. Just over to the track."

"The track? There are no cars over there to park at this hour of the morning."

"I know that. I just want to run around the track a couple of times to loosen up."

The track was a mile around.

"He wasn't a big guy," says Segschneider. "Maybe he was even the smallest of us then, but he was damn strong. He had a big chest and he was tough for a kid his size. I used to take a turn in the ring with him. I never particularly enjoyed it."

Segschneider said he lost track of Redmond when the war started. He knew he had enlisted in the paratroopers, jumped at D-Day, joined the CIA, went to China and died in a prison. All his old friends knew the story.

"I remember him saying once, this was before he joined the service — maybe even before the war, that he had to go where the action was. I guess that's why he joined the CIA. He was a good man. I'm glad I knew him."

Then Segschneider paused for a moment. His voice grew soft. "Tell me one thing," he said. "Do you know how he died? And why?"

Chapter 3

Depression Era Struggle

The big frame house at 309 St. John's Avenue in Yonkers is sixty five years old, the wood cracking on the outside stairs, the paint chipped away by time, the floors inside creaking with every step, the kitchen almost bare except for a small table and two chairs, the bedroom downstairs empty of all furniture, the living room couch a beaten relic of another time.

Richard Falvey, a stocky, redheaded man with deep blue eyes and large, boyish freckles, sits on one of the old wooden chairs in the kitchen. Falvey is married, with three grown children and lives upstate in Hammondsport, New York. He works as a railroad conductor on a freight line and once every two weeks spends a couple of nights alone in his old family house.

"There's nobody left here any more," he says. "I keep trying to sell it but I never quite get around to it. Years ago, after the war, I bought a piece of property in Hammondsport. I loved the land. I wanted a nice house up there with some cows and grass and trees all around. It was a boyhood dream. I wanted to get out of the city. I never thought it would work out. I was finally able to build a home in Hammondsport, and we moved up there. It worked out wonderful. When snow covers the ground in the winter the whole place is just beautiful. I'm a happy man."

When Falvey was a kid, fourteen, fifteen years old, this big old house on St. John's Avenue was sort of a clubhouse for all the kids in the neighborhood. Hughie Redmond and Muggsy Falvey spent a lot of happy hours in the basement of this sprawling four story house.

"We had our boxing ring downstairs and Hughie and me and Jack White used to go at it quite a lot. I was a tough kid — that's how I got the name Muggsy — but Hughie — we called him Coxey — he could hold his own with anybody."

Falvey pulled out a picture from an old photo album. It was a photograph of the Roosevelt High School track team of 1936. A smiling Muggsy Falvey is in the back row — a husky, handsome young man with the varsity "R" of the Roosevelt High School track team on his sweater. Blond, sad-eyed, thin-faced Hughie Redmond, wearing a sweat shirt, is separated from Falvey by two teammates.

"I can't tell you how many years it's been since I looked at this picture. I pulled it out to show it to my kids a few times," Falvey said. "We used to talk about Hughie a lot. Especially during those years when he was in prison. I always thought he would get out. I always told my kids that Hughie would be back and someday they'd get to meet him. He really was an exceptional person, a good friend. I loved Hughie Redmond."

Falvey got up from the table, walked around the small kitchen for a moment, said nothing and sat down again.

"It's funny the things you remember about a guy. Hughie taught me how to drink beer and taught me how to smoke. He would get the guy in the corner candy store to sell him a few cigarettes at a time. An old Jewish man by the name of Mr. Miller ran this store. One day Hughie and I walked in there. There was one thing about Hughie. He had a lot of nerve. He would do things a lot of us were too scared to do. We go into Mr. Miller's store and Hughie goes up to the counter. 'Mistah Millah..." he says in this real Jewish accent..."vot vould you say if I vanted to buy not a pack but von cigarette — just von. Vould you sell me just von, huh, Mistah Millah?' By this time I'm starting to laugh like hell but Hughie keeps going on like this. Mr. Miller is taking it all seriously. After all, this was 1934-35, times weren't all that good you could turn down a sale of even one cigarette. 'Vell, Mistah Millah, vould you give me von?' Miller nodded his head and broke open a pack of Camel's. 'Mistah Millah, you are such a vonderful man, I'll buy five.' Mr. Miller gives him the five cigarettes, Hughie gives him a nickel and Miller thanks him. 'You've velcome, Mistah Millah, I'm sure.' We walk out of the store and Hughie turns to me and says, 'A nice man, dot Mistah Millah, vhy vouldn't you buy von cigarette from him?'"

As a running mate of Redmond's on the Roosevelt High track team, Falvey recalls many conversations about making the Olympics in 1936 as high school boys or certainly in 1940 as college men.

"I think we can make the team for sure in 1940 if we work every day," Redmond said to his pal one frosty morning in the late winter of 1935. "Let's run every morning before school."

Redmond said he would come by Falvey's house the following morning, knock on his window and start their training together with a few laps.

At 5:30 the following morning, with the temperature at eighteen degrees on the small thermometer outside Muggsy Falvey's bedroom window, there was a tapping noise. It grew louder and louder. Falvey stumbled out of bed through the darkness, moved toward the window, cleaned off the frost and stared into the face of Hugh Redmond.

"Let's go, Muggsy," said Redmond.

"Are you crazy? It's freezing out there."

"If you want to make the Olympics you have to train."

"I'll train in the summer."

"Not me. I'm training now. I'm going to do my laps. I'll send you a postcard from Berlin."

Falvey shook his head now in his old house and laughed at the memory.

"Hughie was really determined. I think if he had the money to go on to college he would have made the Olympics. He ran every day, no matter how cold it was. He was good, too. And damn strong, with a hell of a lot of stamina for a little guy. I never saw a guy with such determination, never. Even as a kid he had discipline and patience. That helped him survive later."

Falvey began talking of how good Redmond was at the street game of ring-o-levio, a game played by city kids on the street with circles drawn in chalk, players running in and out trying to tag the player who is "it."

"Guys would run and hide and one by one come out and try to tag the guy in the middle. Everybody would be tagged out in a minute. Hughie always waited until everyone else had been tagged out and he had the stage to himself. Just him and the guy who was in the middle. He could run faster than anybody in our crowd and when he made his move he would run and dodge and beat the other guy in the circle. No matter how long any guy wanted to wait before making a move, Hughie would wait longer. Once in a while a guy would run off, go home, grab a sandwich and a glass of milk and come back. Hughie would still be waiting to be last. He had the patience of a saint."

Falvey's father worked as a surveyor, always making a good living, able to afford the big house on St. John's Avenue and with an extra few bucks for his children.

"Hughie just never got any money from home. His father didn't get paid in that janitor's job and his mother worked all the time. The only money he had was money he saved from odd jobs — parking cars at the track, working as a delivery boy, shoveling snow, things like that.

"We used to go around the neighborhood and hustle soda bottles out of the garbage cans, fill up a wagon and bring them over to the grocery store. We'd get enough money for a movie or a couple of packs of cigarettes. One time Hughie came to me with a book he was reading — he was always reading books — and he saw this big ad for a Charles Atlas course."

"Muggsy," Redmond said, "let's take this Charles Atlas course together."

"What do you have to do?"

"You get exercises to do and a stretching devise to build up your arms and shoulders and an exerciser for your legs. I think it will help us with our running."

"OK, you get it and we can work out in my house."

The Charles Atlas material arrived, complete with books and equipment and was deposited in Muggsy Falvey's basement.

"It was Hughie's stuff, but he didn't want his mother to know that he bought it. She would have thought he wasted his money on nonsense," Falvey said.

The entire basement of Falvey's home was turned over to him for use by the neighborhood kids. There was a pool table, the Charles Atlas equipment, weights, bats and balls and piles of burned out cigarette butts.

Then there were times, as always with Redmond, when he would seem to drop off the face of the earth.

"We always had a routine as kids. It was school and then track practice and then home, playing around my house or in the lot across from Hughie's house. That was about it. Everybody knew where everybody else was. Not Hughie. For no reason and with no explanation," Falvey said, "he would suddenly disappear."

One day, after a week's disappearance from the neighborhood games, he reappeared at Falvey's house to shoot pool.

"Where you been?"

"Home."

"What you been doing?"

"Studying Einstein's theory of relativity."

Falvey picked up the photo of the Roosevelt High track team again and studied the face of Hugh Redmond. Then he turned the photo over and read the names typed on the back.

"Wright...Fesslemieher..Tumauldowsky..Tullke..I bet I haven't thought of some of these guys or mentioned their names for thirty years. It was different with Hughie. He was a very special person. I think he would have been a success no matter what he did. I mean, if he didn't go into the paratroopers and didn't become a CIA guy, he would have succeeded in something else. He was just a bright guy. Look at how he signed his name here."

In a firm, sure hand he had written on this 1935 photo, "Hugh Redmond, Esquire."

Dick Falvey was always close to Redmond, as a kid, and then later on. They served together with the 101st Airborne during the war, he knew Redmond had left home in 1946 to work for the government in China. He followed the prison years in China through the papers and he understood the CIA connection. He didn't understand why Hugh Redmond died.

"I have my theories," he said. "I'm not a politician and I'm not a guy familiar with how the government works. I just know how Hughie Redmond worked. He would have gotten out, he would have made it home, he would be here today if everybody didn't make such a big deal out of it. Hughie Redmond was a guy who knew how to take care of himself. He would have survived if they didn't make him a hero. Hughie Redmond died because people in this town made an important case out of him. The Chinese thought he was more important that he really was. That's why he died. It may not be nice to say but the people who thought they were helping Hughie Redmond helped to kill him."

Of all the names of people in Yonkers who later worked to try to free Hugh Redmond only one man, Vince Sackett, ever really knew Redmond.

Sackett is an older brother of Bobby Sackett. Vince is a tall, thin man who lives with his second wife in a Bronx apartment. He worked for a driver training school. He lived in a house on Borcher Avenue in Yonkers years ago, a few streets down from the Redmond house on Belmont Avenue.

"We moved into that house in 1929. I remember the first time I saw Hugh Redmond, after they moved into the neighborhood, a skinny kid, real frail. I didn't think he could do anything. Then I got to know him. As skinny as he was, as frail as he was, he could do everything other kids could do — and do it better."

Sackett remembers the boxing ring in Dick Falvey's house, the hours spent knocking each other around, the races run and the track events practiced.

"Hughie found his joy in sports. He was a great athlete, a great competitor. He wanted to win. He tried every game there was. He even knew jujitsu. He taught it to me — knocked me on my ass a couple of times before I learned."

Sackett was a practicing Catholic as a young man. He was to go on to study for missionary work at the Maryknoll Fathers order in Maryknoll, New York.

"Hughie's family wasn't interested in the church," Sackett says.

"They weren't interest in politics. They were interested in surviving. That's how things were in those days. The old man worked as a janitor and he got some part time work once in a while in the carpet shop, but I think he kept losing jobs because he would have too much to drink and get into fights with everybody."

Sackett said it was ironic that Redmond would wind up in prison in China with so many missionaries and priests.

"I was a traditional Catholic as a kid. I'm not now because I've seen it from the inside, but I used to wonder, in those days, why everybody didn't go to church. One day I asked Hughie."

"Church is for old women and sick men," Sackett remembers Redmond saying.

Sackett laughed hard as he thought of those words spoken almost sixty years ago by a fifteen year old boy.

"I'm telling you the truth about Hughie Redmond. A lot of people are trying to paint him as something he ain't. He ain't a religious fellow — never was. That was all bullshit. I told you what he said about church, and he never changed his mind. Hughie was a strong-willed guy even when he was a skinny little kid."

Redmond's voice changed earlier than any of his colleagues. It was deeper, more masculine, more mature than any of his friends.

"Hughie liked to sing, too," Sackett remembers. "One day we had a track meet in the lot across from his house — maybe eight, ten of us running some races, pole vaulting, high jumping, broad jumping. We kept our own scores and when it was over we all fell on the ground dead. We were really burned out. Then Hughie stands up and says he is going to serenade us. He begins singing *The Isle of Capri*. Before you know it, we all joined in and he's leading a Yonkers boys' choir."

Redmond never attended church. He made only one exception about church-going.

"He was a ringer in one of the CYO track meets we had in town. We had to meet at the church and he had to pretend he was a member of the church. He did it but he didn't like it. He won the one hundred yard dash and got a medal for it. He was real proud of that," Sackett said.

There was a social center on Yonkers Avenue frequented mostly by Russian and Eastern Europeans, many speaking their native tongues, performing native dances on Friday nights, drinking great quantities of beer, enjoying each other's company in old world surroundings.

"Hughie and I used to go over there a lot," says Sackett. "We were about sixteen or seventeen and we would pick out one of those pretty girls and dance for hours. Hughie would wander off with one of those girls into the deep woods behind the hall. He would be carrying on with one of those girls, bring her back to the hall without so much as a smile, and I'd still be dancing with the same girl I started with. Hughie was a regular guy."

Sackett was studying at Maryknoll during the war. He would see Redmond occasionally back in Yonkers when Redmond was home on furlough.

"Then the war ended and he joined the CIA and I was still at Maryknoll. A lot of our missionaries were sent to China. I remember the last time I saw Hughie Redmond. It was the summer of 1946 and we bumped into each other on the number seven trolley car on the way home. Hughie was getting off, he turned, waved to me and said, 'Vince, I'll see you in Shanghai.'"

Sackett is still bitter about the course of events which followed Redmond's capture.

"They didn't listen to me. If that committee had gone along with me, Hughie Redmond would be alive today. It was run by the politicians in the town. They took it over, they fell in love with the publicity. They didn't give a shit about Hughie Redmond. I did. I loved him. Hughie Redmond had more guts than any of those priests or holy rollers they had in China. He never gave in. That's why we lost him."

Hugh Francis Redmond entered Roosevelt High School in the fall term of 1934 and graduated after the spring term of 1938. the school is a long, low three story brick building on Tuckahoe Road near Central Avenue. It was built in 1925. A large picture of the school's namesake, Theodore Roosevelt, hangs in the front lobby.

Long-haired, noisy boys paraded in and out of the office of the school principal, Dr. Kenneth Fish, one pleasant winter afternoon. Dr. Fish is a tall man, soft spoken, professorial, with thick glasses and sharp features. He looks like Clark Kent.

"Yes, Redmond," he said, with a reserved air. "I've heard of him."

He was concerned about releasing Redmond's school records but agreed after speaking by phone to Redmond's sister.

"We can't let these records out to just anybody," he said.

The worn, white cards were pulled from a file cabinet. A secretary studied the cards carefully before turning them over to Dr. Fish. He examined them with interest.

"Not an exceptional student, I would say," he announced.

The Roosevelt School grade cards had meager information. There was the name REDMOND, HUGH on the top left corner and next to it, I.Q. and the numbers 112 for all his teachers to see, and a notation that he had entered Roosevelt from School Number 4 on September 4, 1934. The rest of the card was a list of his subjects and grades, with no mention of his personality in school, his character or interests. His highest grades were 90s, in gym. His lowest was a 46 in first year Latin. His other failing grades were a 54 in geometry, a 59 in algebra and a 60 in second year Spanish. That became an 80 in third year Spanish. He did well in English, history, civics and biology. His school average was 76, putting him almost directly in the middle of his 1938 graduating class. His major school interests were in track and cross country with four years on the track team and two on the cross country team. His first public mention came in the 1936 Roosevelt High yearbook. Wrote the editor of *L'Envoi* in discussing the track team's prospects for 1936:

> *Looking further down the list of names we find Jack White, Roosevelt's Golden Glover. If White can run as well as he fights the Crimson should be strong in the mile events. Others in the mile event, which is always a strong feature in the city meet, will be Charlie Williams, Hugh Redmond, Eddie Rubinski and Leo Casey.*

A photo accompanying the track article shows Redmond, kneeling in the front row, wearing a gray sweater with the large varsity "R" and gray slacks. His blond hair, worn longer than anyone else's on the team, is combed straight back.

In the spring of 1938, photos for the graduation year book were taken. They show Hugh Redmond, now eighteen and a half years old, fuller in the face, almost handsome, his eyes more friendly and open wider, his blond hair combed in a high neat pompadour, his eyebrows fuller, the cleft in his chin deeply prominent, his full mouth showing the traces of a smile.

The dedication in *L'Envoi* reads:

> *Some of us will go far, many of us, unfortunately, will not.*
> *Successful or not, however, to one and all, the memory of*
> *Roosevelt will return.*

One of the editors of the school yearbook, Larry Spellman, had written of his classmates:

> *Robert Taylor became the girls' favorite actor and our*
> *campus Romeos swore vengeance on him. We took tuber-*
> *culin tests 'cause Mom and Dad made us. Dramatic club*
> *rendered the gay Broadway comedy, "Big Hearted*
> *Herbert."*

Mrs. Mae Henry, a clear-eyed lady of 81, in well deserved retirement after more than 30 years as a teacher in Roosevelt High, remembered Hugh Redmond as a small, thin, blond boy, well disciplined, soft spoken and neat.

"He was in my home room class one year and my English class. In home room they came in, hung up their coats, we took attendance and they went on to their classes. Once a week we had assembly. The boys had to wear ties. I remember he wore the same red tie every week."

Mrs. Henry came to the school when it opened in 1925. She remembers a sister of Theodore Roosevelt being on hand for the dedication.

"We seemed to have more school spirit than they have today. The youngsters cared about the school, they tried to protect its good name," she said.

Was there anything else Mrs. Henry might recall about Hugh Redmond?

"Oh, dear me," she said sweetly, "it is so many years ago. My memory isn't what it used to be. Perhaps if I could find my old marking books I might have a notation in there. I often wrote things down that would help me remember the students when I was grading."

The next day the phone rang.

"I found something," she began. "It was in my grading books for senior English in 1938. All the students were asked to write a long theme. Hugh Redmond's theme was on mental telepathy. Isn't that interesting? Next to his name in the book I had written 'intense eyes.' I remember how serious was the expression on his face. He wasn't a cutup in class. He was a serious student. He seemed like a young man very determined to make something of himself."

On June 22, 1938, Hugh Francis Redmond graduated from Roosevelt High School in Yonkers, New York. He was an average student from an average school in an average city in America. At that moment there seemed little likelihood of anyone outside of his family and close friends ever hearing his name again.

In less than fifteen months circumstances surrounding his life would change dramatically for Hugh Redmond and for millions of people around the world. On September 1, 1939, goose-stepping swastika-carrying disciples of Adolph Hitler and his German National Socialism would invade Poland.

Chapter 4

The End of Innocence

The stock market had crashed in 1929 and the full force of the economic disaster that was to overrun America was being felt severely by the blue collar workers in Yonkers in the early 1930s. Two moves made by the new administration of President Franklin D. Roosevelt helped the Redmonds survive. In 1933, the government created the Civilian Conservation Corps. Then in 1935, the Works Projects Administration came into being,

The senior Hugh Redmond could get no outside work as the Depression deepened. The apartment on Belmont Avenue was rent free in exchange for Redmond's janitorial service. He made no other income for food, for clothing — for any of the other expenses of a growing family with adolescent children. Once a new foreman had taken over at the Alexander Smith carpet factory, Redmond had been able to obtain a day's work on occasion when orders backed up, but by the middle 1930s orders rarely backed up. Ruth Redmond worked at the carpet factory until she was laid off. She began to do housework — cleaning, dusting washing windows and polishing floors in the better neighborhoods of Yonkers. She was paid five dollars a day and given a free lunch.

The WPA saved the Redmond family.

Roosevelt had created the agency to increase jobs, increase purchasing power, and aid families whose major source of income was federal relief. The WPA restored some pride to struggling heads of households. Most important, psychologically, the WPA gave a man a place to go each day, a feeling of some pride, a sense of accomplishment and a reason to go on living with some degree of hope. A man without a job, even a menial job, is a sad shadow of a man, indeed.

The senior Redmond took the WPA job. He helped build roads and repair bridges. He worked on the construction of a Post Office. He helped construct a Federal office building in Yonkers, averaging twenty dollars a week in salary. Ruth Redmond was clearing fifteen dollars a week. With additional federal aid in the form of relief money, they were able to survive and keep their family together.

Young Hugh Redmond graduated from Roosevelt High School in the summer of 1938. Under these oppressive economic conditions he had no idea what he might do with the rest of his life.

"I know he wanted to go to college," says Dick Falvey. "He just didn't think seriously about it because college cost money and kids like us simply didn't have that kind of money. College was for rich kids. That's simply the way it was in 1938."

On the information card he had filled out at Roosevelt High to go with his picture in the yearbook, Redmond had listed Manhattan College as his college choice. He never applied. He could not begin to imagine being able to afford going to Manhattan College. He could not begin to pay for college and all the expenses that implied.

"We often talked about running in the Olympics," says Falvey. "I don't think any of us ever talked about working. Our fathers had trouble getting and holding jobs. How could we get jobs?"

The summer of 1938 was the same for Redmond as the previous three or four summers had been. He played ball and ran track in the lot across the street. He hung out at Bebe's pool hall. He bought cigarettes at Miller's and smoked them in Muggsy Falvey's basement. He drank beer. He made a few bucks parking cars at the race track. He had a few casual romances.

"Somehow or other he saved enough money to buy himself a car," says Ruth Boyle. "It probably cost about twenty or thirty dollars and he got it from one of his pals. It smoked and snorted — one of those old, beat up jalopies, probably a 1932 or '33 Ford that you started yourself. It had that old fashioned crank in the front. He would often call me to come out and turn the key in the ignition while he cranked the starter. I remember the first time he brought it home. He had gone down to have a few beers to celebrate his purchase and show off the car. I think he decided it was a graduation present to himself. Well, he had a couple of beers too many. He drove home, missed the driveway of the house and tore down a fence. The crash practically knocked me out of bed."

Automobile builders, providing mobility for America, did as much for sex with this invention as they did for transportation.

"We would drive around in that old jalopy," says Dick Falvey, "until we picked up a couple of girls. Then it was every man for himself."

One day Redmond and Falvey enticed a couple of young ladies into the car.

"We drove straight over to my house and Hughie let me and one of the girls out," Falvey recalls. "Then he drove off with his date. The next day I asked him how he made out. 'Gee, the funniest thing happened,' he told me. 'We stopped for a couple of beers, drove a little while longer, parked in the woods and had a hell of a time. Then I drove back to my house and the next thing I know I'm waking up in my own bed, with this girl right next to me.' I asked how his mother had taken that. 'Oh, she wasn't upset,' Hugh said. 'I just introduced the girl to her when we got up and she cooked breakfast for all of us.'"

Early in January of 1939, Redmond began looking seriously for work. He applied at the local factories. There were no jobs for unskilled kids with only high school diplomas. He was discouraged. One day he read an article in the paper about the further expansion of a new government work force, the Civilian Conservation Corps, a semi-military government organization labeled the CCC in the press. The CCC provided a job, mostly outdoors, provided uniforms, shelter and food and paid thirty dollars a month. Families on relief were eligible for these jobs.

Young men in the CCCs wore old World War I uniforms, complete with spats and wide-brimmed campaign hats. They were engaged in the conservation of the country's natural resources. They worked in forests and fields. They worked in wildlife preserves and on government flood control projects. The work force was recruited nationally but was assigned mostly to projects in the south and west. There were more than twenty six hundred camps across the country at its peak in 1935, with more than half a million young men between the ages of seventeen and twenty two stationed at the camps. The CCC came under the jurisdiction of the War Department but the men were not technically under military control and could resign at any time. The CCC continued in operation for a short time after the outbreak of World War II and became more deeply involved in projects concerned with military preparedness. Many of the veterans of the semi-military CCC went on to become a cadre in an expanding American armed forces after the United States entrance into World War II.

Redmond applied for the CCC, passed the physical and mental tests and was accepted for employment. On April 1, 1939 he was taken by bus to an upstate New York CCC camp, underwent a short training period, and was then shipped by truck across country to one of the camps at Moab, Utah.

"I remember when he went away," said Vince Sackett. "He was really excited. He had never been out of New York before. He liked the idea that he had a job, that he would be working outdoors and that he could be helping out financially at home. Things were still pretty tough."

The convoy of trucks rumbled through Western Pennsylvania and on into the Midwest, past the outskirts of Chicago, through the farm lands of Illinois, Iowa, Kansas and Nebraska, past roaming wildlife and grazing livestock, over the Rockies in Colorado and across the Colorado River into Utah.

Moab was a rural community, some twelve hundred acres with a population of a little over four thousand. Most of the towns-people were involved in some form of forestry. Felled trees were sent down the Colorado River for use as paper products.

"We were assigned to the same barracks," said George Parnell, a mason who now lives in Los Angeles. "They ran the place like an Army camp. I was in the Army during the war and the CCC got me ready for it. You had a lot of discipline, officers who yelled at you at times and always kept on your tail about the work. Those were tough days. Everybody out there was in trouble financially. We needed the jobs and we put up with a lot. We didn't want to get kicked out and be forced to go home to nothing."

Parnell is a tall man, a shade over six feet, grown fleshy over the years, handsome in an outdoorsy way, with thick black eyebrows and massive hands.

"We worked in forests out there, cutting down trees, clearing fields, planting new trees, loading and unloading timber. Hugh was a strong guy. He fooled me, because he didn't look that strong. We'd start cutting and he proved how strong he was. He was shy at first, maybe trying to prove he could do the work, but then he loosened up. He was a good guy to work with."

There were friendly competitions among the men to see how much work they could do.

"We had four or five guys working together and we would compete against other groups. One of our guys got sick," Parnell recalls. "We were assigned a lesser load because this guy was taken away. Hugh said he didn't think that was right. He said he would do the other guy's work as well as his own. We looked at him like he was nuts. There was enough work for everybody. He insisted so we made our bet with the other guys and went to work. We started chopping and the other group starts chopping. We used to break for lunch on the grass. Redmond didn't break. He just kept hacking away at those goddamn trees as if he hated them. We wound up beating our own total of the day before and winning our bet against the other group, even though we were a man short. Hugh Redmond was one hell of a man."

Parnell had no idea what happened to Redmond after their CCC days. He was not surprised to hear that Redmond was a paratrooper in World War II, but quite surprised to find he had gone into the CIA.

"He was a strong guy, very independent. I could see him as a paratrooper. I was in the engineers myself. That's how I got into masonry. Hugh liked action. He was always on the go. The CIA part surprises me because he seemed to like people — liked to laugh, to drink a beer. Those CIA types seem like quiet guys, always working alone, never telling anybody what they're doing. Maybe he changed after the war."

Parnell remembered that Redmond never talked much about his family and seemed to get less mail than the other guys.

"We knew he was from someplace back east. That was about it. He didn't write many letters. He seemed to do a lot of reading in his spare time, lying on the bunk. Once in a while we would all sing some drinking songs and he would lead us."

Most of the men who got jobs with the CCC were grateful and felt an obligation to repay the government somehow.

"I remember Hugh Redmond saying how Roosevelt was a good man because he cared for the poor people. The war had started in Europe about that time and most of us thought the United States would be dragged in. We figured sooner or later we would all be in the service."

Parnell remembered the boys sitting around their tents one night, playing cards. The talk was about the war in Europe.

"Our conversation stood out in my mind because I heard a lot of guys express the same thoughts later. It seemed unusual then. Redmond said, 'If you gotta die there's no better way to die than fighting for your country.' We were kids then. Hell, we hadn't really lived yet so we weren't willing to think about dying. We laughed at that idea. Hugh Redmond didn't laugh. I remember that. Hugh Redmond was ahead of his time."

The war raged on in Europe. Hitler's armies surged through the Low Countries and into France. Britain was under enormous stress from nightly bombings. The United States, moving inexorably toward war, began a massive buildup of war machines and equipment. Manpower was needed in factories all over the country.

In July of 1940, the CCC camp in Moab, Utah was disbanded and the workers returned home.

"I was walking down the street one day and I passed a guy who looked familiar," said Dick Falvey. "I thought I knew him but I wasn't sure."

"Hey," said Hugh Redmond, "don't you say hello anymore?"

"Is that you, Coxey? I can't believe it!"

Hugh Francis Redmond had gone away to Utah a wiry, callow boy. He had come back a husky man.

"He had developed a huge chest since I'd last seen him," said Falvey. "His arms, shoulders and back had grown enormously. He seemed immense — about twice the size he had been."

"He was really a little too fat," says Ruth Boyle. "He had matured, but he was also eating too much. He was eating my mother out of house and home."

After a month at home, Redmond went out looking for a job. This time he had no trouble. Factories were booming all over Yonkers. He got a job in a factory for thirty five dollars a week. It was more money than his father had ever made at any job.

"We manufactured all kinds of heavy machinery," said Paul Benson, who worked with Redmond. "Hugh could pull those machines around like they were paper."

Benson is a carpenter with a pleasant house on a quiet, tree lined street in a Philadelphia suburb. He weighs nearly two hundred and thirty pounds and stands well over six feet. He is bald, looking a bit like Telly Savalas. He has huge, thick arms and heavy legs. A cigarette dangles from his lips as he talks.

"That was really a boom time in that old plant," he says. "We had more contracts than we could fill. A lot of the married guys would work sixteen or seventeen hours a day. It got so you could work all the overtime you wanted. Guys were bringing home ninety or a hundred bucks a week. Those were the days when milk cost a nickel a container, bread was three cents and you could go to a movie for a dime."

Benson said he had a lot of respect for Hugh Redmond.

"He was a curious guy. He wanted to learn how things worked.

Most guys were given a job in the plant and did it. Redmond did his job — and wanted to know about yours. He kept asking the foreman about the entire project — what part his job would play in the entire machine, where things would go and how the whole thing fit together. He was no factory worker type, you can bet on that. You say he went into the paratroopers and then was in the CIA. Well, let me tell you this. If he didn't have to leave that plant he might have owned the whole damn place in a few years."

Redmond's father, now in his middle fifties, was ailing with arthritis as 1941 began. He had all he could do to keep up with his janitorial chores on the Belmont Avenue building. Ruth Redmond was forced to stay home more and more to care for him on his bad days. Young Ruth was out of school now and working.

In April of 1941, Redmond left the machine factory and moved to a better paying job in Yonkers, at Phelps Dodge Corporation, manufacturers of wire and cables. This job paid fifty dollars a week, and with overtime he was regularly making over a hundred dollars. These were the best of times financially for the Redmonds.

"He always had money in his pocket then," says Ruth Boyle. "He bought new clothes and a better car. He was clearly the man of the house. He would come home from work sometimes with a couple of pounds of shrimp. He loved shrimp. He would stop off on the way home, buy enough for all of us, and bring it in for my mother to cook. He was generous with the money he made."

Phelps Dodge's wire and cable equipment went toward the war effort. Some of the communication wires they manufactured were used on aircraft carriers, some were used on larger ships, some went into the building of bridges and pontoons.

Steven Senita, a man with more than a quarter of a century with the company, said men who worked at Phelps took great pride in knowing their cables were used after D-Day on the Normandy beaches.

"We also manufactured the cables that were laid under the English channel and used for communication," he said.

It was equipment that would help sustain Hugh Redmond and his comrades in France some three years later in the massive invasion of Europe.

"When Hugh worked for us, he always seemed determined to do just a little extra," said Martin Bancroft, a forty year veteran of the company, now retired. "He was that kind of a guy."

Bancroft said they worked the same shift often, pulling cables together, winding them on huge wheels, preparing them for shipment around the world.

"We'd go out after a hard day and have a couple of beers together. Hugh had a good sense of humor — he could laugh, he was a good pal. He would entertain us with a funny story or tell about some wild adventure out west with the CCC. He was a great guy — a smart guy."

Bancroft said there was something else he remembered about Hugh Redmond that might be helpful.

"We were out one night and the guys had a few beers and one of the guys we worked with had one too many. He started riding Hugh about not being in college. 'If you're so damn smart, why aren't you in Harvard?' he was asking. Hugh looked him right in the eye. 'Why the hell don't you mind your own damn business!' I thought they would come to blows, but they didn't. I couldn't figure out why that crack bothered Hugh so much. Then one day he talked to me for the first time about his family — how his father was a janitor, how his mother worked as a maid. He hoped some day he could help them out, get them away from all that. I sort of figured out why he had gotten so upset. The poor guy was embarrassed. How the hell could the son of a janitor even think about college in those days?"

Chapter 5

A Screaming Eagle

It was a crisp Sunday morning in December of 1941. Hugh Redmond sat at the kitchen table of his home at 65 Belmont Avenue reading the sports pages of the *Daily News*. He sipped a cup of coffee and puffed on a cigarette. His father had gone to the basement to work on the furnace. His mother scrubbed one of his work shirts against a washboard, trying to get the factory grime out of it. His sister sewed a dress.

Redmond read with interest the details of the football game to be played at the Polo Grounds in Manhattan that afternoon between the Brooklyn Dodgers and the New York Giants. He had never seen a professional football game and considered going. He wondered if any of the others guys wanted to go to the Polo Grounds with him to see the game. He got up, put on a red plaid windbreaker, put out the cigarette in his saucer and threw the drenched butt in the sink. He turned toward his mother. "I'm going over to Bebe's for a while. Then I'll probably go over to the Polo Grounds for the football game. I'll be home for dinner."

He walked out of his house, turned right on Yonkers Avenue, walked to the corner and moved quickly to Bebe's.

The pool room was filled with cigarette smoke. Three tables were being played. The radio on Bebe's counter was turned to a pop music station. About a dozen young men were in the room. Hughie spotted Bernie Connolly.

"Wanna shoot a rack?" Connolly asked.

"Nah," Redmond said. "I'm going to the football game. Wanna go?"

"Too damn cold to sit out there and freeze your ass. I'm staying here today."

"You see Muggsy around?"

"No, he ain't been in."

The door opened and three young men, strangers, walked into the room. They walked up to the counter and asked for a table. Babe gave them a new chalk, told them they could use table six and handed them a cue ball. Then he turned away.

One of the strangers, a cigarette dangling from his mouth, his jacket buttoned tight, lined up a break shot. The stick moved carefully in his curled fingers three, four, five times, then he broke the rack with a loud crack. Redmond looked over.

"Anybody wanna play a rack for a buck?" asked one of the strangers. He was staring at Redmond.

Redmond looked at him for an instant, reached into his shirt pocket for his cigarettes, lit up a Camel slowly, walked toward the table and nodded his head. "I'll play."

"You can break," the stranger said.

Hugh Redmond walked to the end of the table, chalked up his cue and broke the rack. The balls cracked against the sides as the one ball fell into the side pocket. He moved to the front of the table for another shot. As he was about to hit the cue ball a radio announcement caught his attention.

"Hey, Bebe," Redmond yelled, "turn up the radio."

Bebe moved to the small radio on the shelf, turned it up and walked back to the register.

"Japanese planes have attacked the United States air base at Hickham Field in Pearl Harbor..."

Redmond put down his cue and moved to the front of the hall. He leaned on the table, listening to the voice on the radio.

"Bombers flew over Pearl Harbor at 7:55 this morning, hitting targets on the air field and at the Naval station. Damage is reported to be heavy."

The radio reports continued as most of the young men in the pool hall moved close to the radio to listen. It didn't take long for them to realize that this attack by Japan meant war. The United States would soon be in the war and all of these young men, including Hugh Francis Redmond, would have their lives dramatically changed by that attack on Hawaii. Redmond was prepared.

He had just turned twenty two years old, a healthy, strong, athletic young man with decent high school grades, a clean record in the CCC and a fine record as a factory worker. He was also single. All this put him in position to be selected quickly for the draft, sure to be heavily accelerated now that the United States was in the war.

Redmond had become the major support of his family. His father, deteriorating from arthritis, had all he could handle just doing his janitorial chores. The other tenants gave him nothing but grief. His mother and sister could contribute little money to the household.

He thought about enlisting. He knew his number would soon come up in the draft. He discussed it with his mother. All decisions in the Redmond home now were made by mother and son. His father was growing old, tired, weakened by illness and worn out by his work. He was depressed in mood, often falling asleep at night in his chair after a few beers. Small, frail and near-sighted, Redmond's mother was a woman of strong will. She didn't think it was right for her son to enlist in the service immediately given their situation at home. She wanted him to wait and see how the war went — wait and see if he could retain his dependency deferment, wait to see what developed.

The Phelps Dodge plant moved quickly into heavy defense work. Money was plentiful and the total number of employees jumped from seven hundred in 1940 to more than two thousand early in 1942.

"We worked around the clock," said Steven Senita. "We never lacked for work. We only lacked people to do the work."

Redmond would often work an extra shift for the money. He did heavy work on the cables and also drove the small panel truck with equipment to various parts of the plant, bringing cable and wire to complicated jobs.

The war news was bad. The Japanese swept through the South Pacific. They gained victory after victory, driving the United States out of the Philippine Islands as General Douglas MacArthur escaped to Australia. They conquered Corregidor and killed and captured many Americans and Filipinos, defeating the American fleet at the massive battle of Java Sea, driving deep into New Guinea and threatening Australia.

In Europe the news for the Allies was just as bad. Rommel marched triumphantly through North Africa. The Luftwaffe flew with complete freedom over most of Europe. The German Army pushed deep into Russia and, scattering Russian patrols, penetrated the gates of Stalingrad. The summer of 1942 was the low point of the war for the Western democracies.

The full effect of the war on this country, seeping down to local neighborhoods, was being felt. Yonkers underwent dramatic changes. The city prepared for attack. Air raid drills were held often. Children huddled under their coats in the school halls. Air raid wardens wore helmets with civil defense emblems on them. Windows were painted black. Shades were pulled every night to keep light from seeping out. The sounds of airplanes brought fear. Certain products began disappearing from store shelves. Rationing of food and gasoline was instituted. Coffee was difficult to obtain. Sugar, butter, meat and cooking oil became scarce. Gasoline was hard to get and automobile tires had to be repaired, regardless of how worn they were. No replacements were available.

The young men from Yonkers were being drafted in greater numbers. Many were enlisting, especially high school students upon their graduation in June of 1942. Neighborhood youngsters were organized by civic and church groups to send letters to their relatives and friends in the Army, Navy, Marines and Air Corps. They were given badges for letters as members of the Write-A-Fighter Corps. Enlistment posters filled the streets and enlistment stations appeared everywhere. More and more young men were disappearing from the streets.

War casualties shocked the community. One young Yonkers Marine was killed in the Philippines. Another died in the crash of a Navy fighter in the Pacific. The son of a well known teacher was burned to death in a Japanese bombing attack on his aircraft carrier.

In early August, Dick Falvey and Hugh Redmond sat in Bebe's pool hall, sipped a beer, smoked and talked quietly.

"I've decided to enlist in the paratroopers," said Falvey. "The Army will get me soon anyway. This way I can choose."

"I've been thinking about the same thing," Redmond said. "My father seems a little better."

"I'm going down tomorrow to join up."

"I'll have to figure out how my folks will get along without me," Hugh said.

"Let me know what you decide," Falvey said. "Maybe we can go in together."

"If we go in, we might as well go where the action is."

"That's what I figure."

They had a couple more beers, talked a few more minutes and then went their separate ways.

The following afternoon Richard Falvey walked into the main Post Office in Yonkers and enlisted in the United States Army for training as a paratrooper. Hugh Redmond went to work that day as usual at Phelps Dodge.

"Hughie had this incredible loyalty to his family," Falvey said. "He had a deep sense of obligation. I think he wanted to go when I did, but he didn't want to leave until he knew that his family could manage without him."

Three weeks later, Dick Falvey left Yonkers for basic training with the 101st Airborne at Camp Toccoa, Georgia.

✳

"...a parachute must permit slow descent, must be of little weight and small area, must retain its shape in descent and not become unbalanced, and must be of good stability. A parachute consists, in general, of a flexible material which when extended takes the form of an umbrella and from which a series of cords converge downward to a harness strapped to the user. Before the

parachute is inflated the user must wait until he is well
clear of the aircraft in order to avoid entanglement, or
fouling. The harness must be easily detached when the
earth's surface is reached, since the parachutist might be
drowned or injured by dragging along the ground. The
rate of descent for a man-carrying parachute is about 18
feet per second."

The Columbia Encyclopedia — 3rd Edition

Man has long been fascinated with flying. Adventurous men envied the birds and tried to repeat their skills to gain the same freedom. Greek mythology recounts the story of Icarus, a young man who attempted to escape his enemies in Crete by flying with wings made for him by his father Daedalus. Heady with the joy of flight, he flew so close to the sun that his wings, made of feathers and wax, melted and he fell to his death in the Aegean Sea.

Always, there has been the dream of flight and dreams of escape. Some dreamed of a craft in the sky. More creative men dreamed of escaping from such a craft, feeling the winds in his very soul, soaring easily, seeing the curve of the earth beneath him. These dreams of flight, these advanced dreams of falling free, were always in the minds of men.

In 1784 Benjamin Franklin had written, "Where is the Prince who can afford so to cover his country with troops for its defense, as that ten thousand men descending from the clouds might not, in many places, do an infinite deal of mischief before a force could be brought together to repel them?"

In 1785 a French balloonist by the name of Jean Pierre Blanchard claimed the invention of the parachute. In 1797, another French balloonist named Jacques Garnerin dropped three thousand feet from a balloon in the first successful descent through space. Balloonists continued to leap from the skies for more than a century — sometimes with tragic results.

On December 17, 1903, on a windswept field near Kitty Hawk, North Carolina, a bicycle mechanic named Orville Wright, working with his brother Wilbur, flew twelve seconds in the first controlled, sustained flight in a power driven airplane. The age of flight was upon man. Parachutists would now be leaping from thousands of feet instead of hundreds, from fast moving airplanes instead of from hot air balloons and gliders.

As a weapon of war, a means of delivering men and material to far away battle fields, the parachute came into early use in minor ways in World War I. The Germans used it again extensively in Spain in 1937 and began making great use of its potential with the outbreak of World War II. German paratroopers were considered an elite branch of Hitler's war machine.

Americans had experimented with parachute training during the 1930s. There were few planes to jump from and fewer men skilled in the art of parachuting as the United States entered World War II. Parachute units were to be formed and training accelerated early in 1942. On August 16, 1942, under the command of Major General William C. Lee, a skilled parachutist, a new parachute division was created.

General Lee — tall, handsome, square jawed, a ringer for movie cowboy actor Randolph Scott, stood on a reviewing platform at Camp Clairborne, Louisiana on a sweltering summer afternoon, looked down upon the young men of his division and told his new Screaming Eagles..."The 101st Airborne Division has no history, but it has...a rendezvous with destiny."

Units of smaller strength, regiments, battalions, companies, had been formed throughout the summer of 1942 to make up the full force of this new division. The 506th Parachute Infantry Regiment, under the command of Lieutenant Colonel Robert F. Sink, a mustachioed West Pointer, class of 1927, had been activated at Toccoa, Georgia on July 20, 1942.

Red-headed, freckle-faced Richard Falvey of Yonkers, New York, was assigned to headquarters company, second battalion, 506th Parachute Infantry Regiment of the 101st Airborne Division upon his arrival in Georgia.

That afternoon, after more than a week of serious thought on the matter, Hugh Francis Redmond of Yonkers, New York, walked into his main Post Office branch and enlisted in the United States Army for training as a paratrooper.

On September 12, 1942 Redmond was inducted into the Army, taken from the Manhattan Induction Center on Whitehall Street by bus to Fort Dix, New Jersey, issued uniforms, examined, briefed, lectured, given a crew cut, punctured with needles, fed his first Army meals (including his first breakfast of creamed chipped beef on toast, forever enshrined by millions of GIs as shit on a shingle, or S.O.S.), yelled at constantly by swollen sergeants, awakened violently each morning by the pounding of clubs on his aluminum bed, issued dog tags and identification cards, taken by truck to a railroad station and sent by troop train to join the 101st Airborne at Camp Toccoa, Georgia. He was assigned to headquarters company, third battalion, 506th Parachute Infantry Regiment of the 101st Airborne. There were one hundred and eighty men, mostly raw recruits like himself, in each of the fifteen companies of the 506th Parachute Infantry Regiment.

"It was raining like hell and we had a five minute break," recalls Dick Falvey. "I ran to the latrine. I looked up as I was racing across the field and there was Hugh Redmond. We talked for a minute, made up to have a beer together when we got a minute off and went our separate ways. I knew Hughie would eventually join us. There was never a guy better qualified for the paratroopers."

Paratrooper training seemed to have been devised by sadists. In fact, it was devised by brilliant soldiers who knew what rigors one must overcome to survive as a paratrooper. Toccoa was a piece of barren, hot dusty land in the middle of nowhere — the only landmark being a mountain range that reached high into the blue Georgia sky. It was three miles up and three miles down the winding trails of Mount Currahee. The troops would get to know every inch of it.

Troopers were trained to march the trails in fifty minutes, to move with full packs at one hundred and thirty paces per minute on twenty mile forced marches, to stretch and strengthen their bodies and muscles, to do a hundred pushups and twenty chin-ups, to scale wooden barriers, to move quickly, hand over hand, through ladder lifts, to crawl on their knees with logs in their arms, to push their mental and physical capacity beyond known limits. Some puked. All bitched and many dropped out, reassigned out of the paratroopers, destined to forever know they had failed the greatest challenge of their young lives. The survivors grew stronger, more able, more proud, more together with each passing day. Competition grew keener between men, between squads and platoons, between companies, battalions and regiments, working its way up to the competition that was to profit all concerned between the 82nd Airborne Division and the 101st Airborne Division.

In some thirteen weeks of vigorous training the twenty one hundred men of the 506th became solders, tough, strong, capable, rugged fighting men. Now they were to become paratroopers.

They would start with nomenclature, learning the various parts and functions of a parachute. Their lives might well depend on how they learned. They would move to the rigs, jumping off long wooden tables at first, reciting over and over again, sometimes in their sleep, the five points of performance..."check body position and count...get your back into the wind...prepare to land...and land."

Then, getting higher off the ground, moving up, at the mock tower, a large piece of canvas over a small wooden platform, some sixty feet in the air, the shout of "GO," and a violent sensation of being dropped and caught by a wire, the jerk upwards, the sense of relief, the soft sweet feeling of floating down gently to the ground.

The training grew tougher. More calisthenics, longer hours of practice, more sit-ups and pushups, less sleep, more night patrols, more marching, marching, marching. The paratroopers of the 506th Parachute Infantry Regiment had not yet jumped from an airplane. They were building for their moment.

Early in December of 1942, on a miserable winter morning, with steady rain and a thick blanket of fog, the second battalion of the 506th moved out of Toccoa to Five Points, Georgia — some one hundred and twenty miles away. They marched through ankle deep mud and over hilly terrain. They marched through bitter winds and over icy patches, frozen fields and on slick roads. Their socks froze and their shoes grew heavier by the minute. They carried upwards of sixty pounds of equipment on their backs and covered the one hundred and twenty miles in a little more than four days.

"Now I know why the paratroopers of Uncle Sam's Army prefer to be called the Parachute Infantry," wrote reporter Odom Fanning in the *Atlanta Journal*. "Fair weather or foul, their job is one percent parachuting and ninety nine percent old fashioned marching and fighting."

The forced march beat the best known records of German and Japanese troops and Colonel Sink, effusive over his regiment's performance, called the military achievement "unparalleled in continental American history." Paratroop commanders were as adept at public relations as they were to later prove adept in combat. The troopers had given the entire country an important boost to morale.

The troops had marched across Georgia from Toccoa to the outskirts of Atlanta. After resting they moved on through the city, boarded trains and rolled on through the countryside of Georgia to Fort Benning. Serious training as paratroopers would continue there.

"We were young, we were kids, really. We had a lot of spirit," recalls Dick Falvey. "We had never been tested before and it was interesting to find out just how good we were as men."

The record lasted about as long as it took the third battalion, including Private Hugh Redmond, to march from Toccoa to Fort Benning, a distance of some one hundred and thirty six miles, covered in less than four days. They were led personally by Major Robert Wolverton, West Point, class of 1937, a husky six footer from Elkins, West Virginia. Major Wolverton, unaccustomed to marching on ice and mud with his troops, had to finish the journey in the back of an ambulance after blood from his feet seeped through his boots onto the Georgia highway.

At Fort Benning, soldiers became paratroopers. The training intensified. Bodies were toughened. More practice on the mock tower, then on to a higher tower. Finally, after some seventeen weeks of long days and dark nights, of a strange mixture of bravado and fear, of pain and pleasure, the word came. JUMP.

The men were lined up one cold morning in full equipment, piled into trucks and driven to Lawson Field, emptied out and marched in single file to waiting C-47s. None of the recruits had ever jumped from an airplane. Few had ever actually been up in an airplane. In minutes, they were aloft. The planes reached cruising altitude and from the height of one thousand feet they were to stand up and hook up. They checked their static lines, aided their buddies in front and back, the plane doors were opened and away they went. More than seventeen hundred and fifty young parachute school trainees, more than ten per minute were falling from the sky — their arms outstretched now — their knees slightly bent, the earth moving up at them rapidly from never before seen angles.

"Nobody ever minds the first jump very much," says Dick Falvey. "It's the second one that makes you sick."

The entire regiment jumped without a fatality. Less than one percent of the men who boarded the C-47s that December morning failed to jump. The average in other units had run as high as twenty five percent.

On December 18, 1942, Colonel Sink addressed his assembled soldiers on the drill field at Fort Benning. He read from a memorandum he had prepared for the occasion:

MEMORANDUM TO THE SOLDIERS OF THE 506TH
PARACHUTE INFANTRY:

You have now become qualified parachutists and wear the wings of the parachute soldier. You are a member of one of the finest regiments in the United States Army, and, consequently, in the world. You must keep in mind that first you are a soldier in the Army of the United States: that you are a parachutist, the elite of this army, and finally you are a member of the 506th Parachute Infantry.

Parachute wings were pinned on the members of the 506th and they were sent home on furlough. They were to reassemble after fourteen days at Camp Benning early in January of 1943.

When they returned they were trucked to Alabama for intensive maneuvers, learned house to house combat, then moved north for more training at Camp Mackall near Hoffman, North Carolina. They lived in new barracks, ate in large mess halls, and weekended in small North Carolina towns. More night training lay ahead. On one such night, the star-crossed Colonel Wolverton was captured by "enemy" troops, tied to a tree and had his jeep stolen. More jumps followed. A soldier by the name of Joe Operowski was killed in a practice jump when he landed poorly and broke his neck — the first 506th fatality. Training continued uninterrupted. Maneuvers were held in North Carolina, Georgia, Tennessee and Alabama. The regiment was moved again to Fort Bragg and on April 10, 1943, the entire 101st Airborne, now at full strength, was reviewed by the Commanding General, William C. Lee and his guest, film star Dick Powell.

By the middle of 1943 the Germans and Japanese had been slowed down almost everywhere. The Allies were on the offensive. North Africa had been retaken. The German drive into Russia was stalled at the gates of Stalingrad. American production was outstripping the enemy war machine. The war was about to reach its decisive stage. American forces were preparing for the biggest invasion in the history of war. The finest young men of the United States would soon embark on an invasion that would save Europe and change the world.

Chapter **6**

Training For a Moment in History

Robert Webb is sixty nine years old, a gregarious salesman of X-ray equipment who lives with his wife and four children in Houston, Texas.

Ray Calendrella is sixty eight years old, a soft spoken bachelor from Hamden, Connecticut who worked as a court reporter.

James Bradley, sixty eight years old, married, the father of four children, worked in the trust department of a bank and lives in San Fernando, California.

William Pauli is sixty nine years old, married, with four sons and operates his own machine shop business in Valier, Montana, a town of some six hundred people.

These four men were all members of Headquarters Company, Third Battalion of the 506th Parachute Infantry Regiment of the 101st Airborne Division and served with Hugh Redmond from their beginning training at Camp Toccoa, Georgia to England, France, Belgium and Holland.

"I can hear his voice even now," said Webb. "Redmond had one of those voice you wouldn't forget. I guess it was his accent. You know how guys from New York talk with all that slang and New Yorkese? This guy was like that. There was one other thing. He could talk out of the side of his mouth like a race track tout. He must have spent a lot of time around race tracks in his day."

"I remember this one time in a beer hall called Scotty's in North Carolina," said Bill Pauli. "There were some guys in there from the 508th. Somebody passed some remark about guys in the 506th. I was sitting there minding my own business and all of a sudden Redmond jumped up and knocked this guy across the room. Now a big brawl breaks out. Everybody had a good old time. Scotty's was put off limits to the 506th after that."

"Redmond was an original member of our company," said Jim Bradley. "I looked at this old picture of our company to recall his face. He's up in the second row — not a big guy, but a guy I remember who knew his way around."

Paratroopers developed a fierce pride in this fraternity, in their skills, enjoyed the privileges of jump boots and bloused pants, made sure the rest of the Army knew they made the most money with the fifty dollars a month extra they were paid as jump pay (one hundred dollars a month for officers) and pressed the point to outsiders that each and every one of them was a volunteer.

"Troopers were very independent guys," said Pauli. "I was made the acting sergeant of our platoon, a communications platoon. Redmond was a radio operator. He worked under me. He would give you a little static at times when you told him to do something. He wouldn't take heat from anybody. He was a strong-willed person. He was proud to be a trooper. He made all his jumps. One time we had this big guy in the outfit, maybe six feet five or six, probably went two hundred and thirty pounds at least, and we were practicing night jumps from the tower. They just called out names and guys would move up the ladder in turn. This big guy didn't like jumping. He was just plain scared. They called off this guy's name and he just froze. They called it again and Redmond, who had already jumped, moved right in and climbed the ladder. We all knew what was going on but the officer didn't. It was funny because this guy was the biggest guy in our group and Redmond probably was the smallest. Maybe the toughest, too."

The days at Camp Shanks, some thirty miles north of New York City, passed slowly for the men of the 506th. There were formations just for the sake of formations, inspections at all times, the common Army boredom of hurry-up-and-wait syndrome at mess halls, shot lines, equipment lines. Restless hours were passed at the gym, the movies, at the old desks in day rooms used for last minute letter writing or reading.

The men were impatient about moving on. They knew they were on their way to war, but at least that would be exciting. Sitting around an embarkation port could be a lot worse than getting shot at.

Finally the word came that the 506th was moving out. There were the last minute checks on gear, last minute equipment changes, uniforms cleaned, boots shined, packs arranged for the trip. The men were awakened at 3:30 one dark morning and ordered to assemble in the company street with full packs, all equipped and ready to leave. They were marched in the dark to waiting trucks and boarded the two and a half ton open trucks, packed in tightly and wheeled quickly onto the highway. The 506th was moving down the country roads under cover of night to New York City.

When they arrived in the city they continued to move to the docks, boarding a large converted ocean liner named the *Samaria* for the journey across the sea to England. They boarded, giving their names, rank and serial numbers as officers stood alongside the clerks, checking that all men on their rosters were on hand.

The ship set sail at daybreak and the men of the 506th were able to see the Statue of Liberty fading in the early light as the journey began. They were moving out to the open sea now, these brave young men, off to strange lands with strange names, off to fight for their country.

Soon many of them forgot their noble mission as they grew seasick, battling constant nausea and a desire to be dead.

"The only thing that made the trip tolerable," remembers Dick Falvey, "was knowing it would be over in ten or eleven days." Falvey passed the long hours sleeping, reading, playing cards and dreaming of a good meal.

"I saw Hugh Redmond twice on board the *Samaria*. The first time he was in a big crap game his guys had going. He told me he was up seven hundred dollars. Then I didn't see him again for another five or six days. I finally ran into him in a corner of the deck. He was sitting against a rail with a small pad and pencil in his hand."

"You writing home?" Falvey asked.

"Nope. I'm working on something," Redmond said.

"What is it?"

"Speedwriting. I figure if I can devise this speedwriting code for myself I can save a hell of a lot of time when I have to write letters. If you eliminate most of the endings on words you can cut down the writing time to about half and still understand what you're saying."

Falvey said Redmond tried to show him how his system worked. "He could always find something to keep his mind busy. I never ever heard him complain about being bored."

On September 7, 1943 the *Samaria* was off the coast of Ireland, steaming north and east through St. George's Channel, docking at Liverpool, England. Bands welcomed the ship, dock workers waved to the troops and pretty girls studied them. They were soon disembarking, struggling again with their duffel bags, piling into waiting trucks and rolling toward the train station. They moved by train across the English countryside, passing through picture postcard pretty little villages, through the ruins of some bombed out towns, getting a clear message of why they had crossed the Atlantic.

Third battalion was stationed in the quiet country town of Ramsbury in southern England, little more than an hour by rail from London. They moved into spacious wooden barracks, shielded for the most part from residents of the town by tall trees. Other members of the 101st were stationed at small towns nearby — Aldbourne, Chilton Foliat, Froxfield, Chiseldon and Swindon.

In a few days, after getting accustomed to their new surroundings and the English weather, training resumed for the 506th, increasing in intensity. There was the night work, more field problems, more work in map reading, using the compass, a study of the natural terrain for help in directional guidance. The regiment "attacked" endless towns, hills and wooden areas in England, simulating combat conditions, digging foxholes, learning to live in these shallow pits of earth, making do with small amounts of water and K rations. Range firing continued. Jumps were held often. Troops worked hard on freeing themselves rapidly from their chutes upon landing, then taking cover. The night jumps, the long forced marches, the endless hours of working on equipment and long hours of body building worked these men into hardened athletes as well as fighting solders. When the time came, they would be ready to cross the Channel into France.

After several weeks in the camps the men were allowed to go on weekend pass. Redmond, Falvey and several of the other men of the 506th took buses into London, visited the famous sites of the town, took pictures in front of Big Ben, visited Parliament, walked the back streets, checked out a number of pubs and made friends with the locals girls, enjoying their excursions like any tourists.

As the 506th established its bases and the soldiers became part of the neighboring communities, their early feelings of strangeness began to disappear. The soldiers became comfortable visiting the local pubs. The locals visited the men of the 506th at their bases. After some time, tradesmen were allowed on to the bases at specified times to sell to the GIs.

One of the popular tradesmen was a truck driver who brought bakery goods. One Sunday morning, when Hugh Redmond was confined to the base by a scheduled late hour guard duty, he chanced to walk through an open area and spotted the bakery truck. He saw a pretty girl standing next to the truck, holding a tray of hot rolls. She walked into the officers' quarters and soon came back to the truck to check her stock. Redmond walked over to the truck as she came back from her delivery.

"Hi. My name is Hugh Redmond. Do you have any rolls I can buy?" he said.

"Oh. Yes. Certainly. My father is on the truck and I think he might have an extra tray. Is it for your barracks?"

"No, it's for me."

The kid with the New York accent and the girl from Ramsbury found out how easy it was to understand each other. They began meeting regularly.

Mrs. Sylvia Benning Brown, a lovely lady of seventy one, with traces of gray in her brown hair, is a grandmother now, the wife of a Ramsbury shopkeeper, mother of four grown children, two of whom are married with children of their own. She speaks warmly of her relationship with Hugh Redmond in the early days of 1944, when she was an eighteen year old school girl.

"He was a very nice young man, very gentle. We used to laugh a lot together at how strange his manner of talking was. He would tease me by trying to talk with a British accent and I would try to talk like a New Yorker to him. My father had the bakery during the war. I worked there after school and on weekends and was often in the camp delivering trays of sweets. Late Saturday and most of Sunday we would meet and walk through the woods together, Hugh and I."

Each day, when Sylvia Denning brought her trays to the camp, Hugh Redmond would leave messages for her under a large tree. The messages were coded in Redmond's shorthand. He had worked hard to teach Sylvia his secret code.

"It was a delightful game we played," she said. "We would make plans to meet each other late Saturday. Then we would just enjoy a walk, look at the trees, talk about New York — what it was like and how much I wanted him to show it to me when the war was over."

After the 506th left Ramsbury there was no contact between Sylvia Banning and Hugh Redmond ever again.

"It was simply one of those typical little wartime flings. We enjoyed each other's company. We were never serious about anything except having fun. My word, we were both so young then. So many of those American soldiers would make incredible promises and tell incredible stories about their lives back in the United States. They broke a lot of hearts when they left. Hugh never did that. He was kind, decent, a fine young man. I liked him a great deal."

Sylvia was not surprised when told that Hugh Redmond had become a CIA agent after the war, had gone to China, had died in a Chinese prison because he wouldn't tell the Chinese what they wanted to hear.

"Hugh was a wonderful person to know," she said. "He was a gentleman at all times. He loved those codes he made up and tried to teach me. It was so many years since I thought of him. I'm glad to know what happened to him. We had many happy days together."

*

On March 14, 1944 the 101st Airborne Division lost its division commander, General William C. Lee. He suffered a massive heart attack while working long hours on invasion plans, and was sent back to the States for treatment.

The new commanding general of the 101st Airborne Division was a handsome, ramrod-straight, forty-three-year-old West Pointer (class of 1922) from Keytesville, Missouri, named Maxwell Davenport Taylor. Brigadier General Taylor had been serving as Chief of Staff and Artillery Commander of the 82nd Airborne Division when he received his new orders.

Promoted now to Major General, Taylor conferred with his chief aides upon arrival at 101st headquarters, General Anthony McAuliffe, General Gerald Higgins and General Dan Pratt, with 506th commander Colonel Sink, with other 506th officers including Colonel Charles Chase, Colonel Robert Strayer, Colonel William Turner, Major Louis Kent, Colonel James LaPrade, Colonel Robert Wolverton, Colonel Lloyd Patch, Major Oliver Horton, Colonel Clarence Hester and Colonel Charles Shettle. The mission was getting closer.

In early April of 1944, with the weather breaking and some soft clouds filling the sky, the 506th put on a brilliant exhibition of combat jumping on an open English field. Targets were marked on the ground and hit. Paratroops were out of their chutes rapidly, assembling on command, the movement smoothly timed, organized and executed to perfection.

Prime Minister Winston Churchill, wearing a long dark coat and a bowler hat, the ever present cigar stuck in his mouth and carrying a cane in his right hand, stood on a high platform and watched the smoothly executed routines. Others on the reviewing platform included the Supreme Allied Commander, General Dwight David Eisenhower, Lieutenant General Omar Bradley, General Taylor, General Pratt, General McAuliffe, assorted American and British observers and a battery of reporters and cameramen.

Before going aloft the paratroopers had assembled near the Prime Minister, who stood bareheaded in a jeep. They had raced with battle standards and flags flying, cheering wildly, laughing and yelling after General Eisenhower had ordered them to break ranks and visit with

Churchill. The Prime Minister talked with many of them, shook hands, and wished them well. Each man seemed thrilled and excited in the presence of this heroic figure.

Then they jumped and Churchill, making his first full scale inspection of American troops, was to call the men of the 506th "The most modern expression of war." He would tell them later, "Soon you will have the opportunity of testifying to your belief in all those great phrases embodied in the American Constitution. I thank God you are here," he continued, "and from the bottom of my heart I wish you all good fortune and success."

The pressure built each day. The training was at its most intense. Rumors swept through the camps. It would be soon — that grand and glorious day when the skies would be filled with paratroopers and the Germans would retreat in their wake. When? Where? The German defense seemed less important than the tides across the English Channel. Tides were controlled by the moon and tides controlled the beaches. The landings had to be carried out during low tide. Each day became more difficult for the men as rumors flew through the camps. The men of the 506th were well prepared, well trained, as ready as they would ever be to show off the skills they had worked to sharpen for so many months.

The days moved slowly.

Redmond family photos of Hugh as youngster at Yonkers home.
(Redmond Family Photos)

Hugh in the CCCs
before World War II,
(above left), with his
parents and sister while
on leave from duty with
the 101st Airborne
Division (above right),
and at Ward Road
Prison in Shanghai,
China in 1962 (right).
(Redmond Family
Photos)

Hugh, second row right, on 1936 Roosevelt High School Cross Country team. (top). 1937 Cross Country team at Roosevelt High School, Hugh, lower right corner (center photo). (Roosevelt High School photos)

Roosevelt High School as it looks today (left). (Author's photo)

Two Redmond family homes in Yonkers — 65 Belmont Avenue (right) and 19 Intervale Place (below). (Author's photo)

Army of the United States

SEPARATION QUALIFICATION RECORD

SAVE THIS FORM. IT WILL NOT BE REPLACED IF LOST

This record of job assignments and special training received in the Army is furnished to the soldier when he leaves the service. In its preparation, information is taken from available Army records and supplemented by personal interview. The information about civilian education and work experience is based on the individual's own statements. The veteran may present this document to former employers, prospective employers, representatives of schools or colleges, or use it in any other way that may prove beneficial to him.

1. LAST NAME—FIRST NAME—MIDDLE INITIAL	MILITARY OCCUPATIONAL ASSIGNMENTS		
REDMOND, HUGH F.	10. MONTHS	11. GRADE	12. MILITARY OCCUPATIONAL SPECIALTY

2. ARMY SERIAL NO.	3. GRADE	4. SOCIAL SECURITY NO.	10. MONTHS	11. GRADE	12. MILITARY OCCUPATIONAL SPECIALTY
12 142 403	Cpl	099 16 6882	3	Pvt	Inf. Basic (521)
5. PERMANENT MAILING ADDRESS (Street, City, County, State)			18	Pvt	Radio Operator Low Speed (7776)
65 Belmont Ave. Yonkers, West Chester Co. N. Y.			15	Cpl	Wire Chief Tel & Tel (7261)

6. DATE OF ENTRY INTO ACTIVE SERVICE	7. DATE OF SEPARATION	8. DATE OF BIRTH
12 Sep 1942	18 Oct 1945	30 Oct 1919

9. PLACE OF SEPARATION
Separation Center, Cp Blanding, Fla.

SUMMARY OF MILITARY OCCUPATIONS

13. TITLE—DESCRIPTION—RELATED CIVILIAN OCCUPATION

RADIO OPERATOR, LOW SPEED—Installed and operated tactical field radio transmitting and receiving equipment for a Parachute Infantry Battalion in England, France, Belgium and Holland. Sent and received messages by International Morse Code CW and tone signals. Received and transmitted CW and Tone signals, using hand key. Performed maintenance by inspection, cleaning, repair, and adjustment of equipment.

WD AGO FORM 100
1 JUL 1945

This form supersedes W D AGO Form 100, 15 July 1944, which will not be used.

MILITARY EDUCATION

14. NAME OR TYPE OF SCHOOL—COURSE OR CURRICULUM—DURATION—DESCRIPTION

Attended Parachute Jump School, Ft. Benning, Ga. for 4 weeks, learning parachute jump techniques and packing of parachute. Attended advanced communications School at Ft. Benning, Ga. for 6 weeks learning how to install and operate a low speed radio.

CIVILIAN EDUCATION

15. HIGHEST GRADE COMPLETED	16. DEGREES OR DIPLOMAS	17. YEAR LEFT SCHOOL	OTHER TRAINING OR SCHOOLING	
4 yrs. H.S.	Diploma	1938	20. COURSE—NAME AND ADDRESS OF SCHOOL—DATE	21. DURATION
18. NAME AND ADDRESS OF LAST SCHOOL ATTENDED			NONE	
Roosevelt High School Yonkers, New York				
19. MAJOR COURSES OF STUDY				
Academic				

CIVILIAN OCCUPATIONS

22. TITLE—NAME AND ADDRESS OF EMPLOYER—INCLUSIVE DATES—DESCRIPTION

HOISTING ENGINEER—Operated a 30 ton electric hoist in a cable factory, Dodge & Phelps Corp., Yonkers, N.Y., from 1940 to 1942. Carried cable from place to place during manufacture. Knew braking, starting, stopping, cable reeling, and travelling.

ADDITIONAL INFORMATION

23. REMARKS

NONE

24. SIGNATURE OF PERSON BEING SEPARATED	25. SIGNATURE OF SEPARATION CLASSIFICATION OFFICER	26. NAME OF OFFICER (Typed or Stamped)
Hugh F. Redmond	Arthur S. Farber	ARTHUR S. FARBER 1st Lt. AGD

Redmond U.S. Army separation papers after service with the 101st Airborne Division. (front of document above, back of document right).

VETERANS ADMINISTRATION
Form P-80 a—Rev. May 1944

FILE No. C-5,851,945
Adj-214

AWARD OF DISABILITY COMPENSATION OR PENSION
(SERVICE CONNECTED)
December 6, 1945.

TO: Mr. Hugh F. Redmond, Jr.
65 Belmont Ave.,
Yonkers, N. Y.

Dear Sir:

In accordance with the provisions of __Public #2, 73rd Congress, as amended__ you are hereby notified that as a __Cpl. Hq.Co. 2nd Bn 4th Inf. TFS__ , who was discharged from the __military__ service of the United States on the __18th__ day of __October__ 19__45__, you are awarded __pension__ in the amount of __$11.50__ from __October 19,__ , __1945__, on account of disability resulting from the following conditions held to have been incurred or aggravated during your __War Service__
(War or regular service)

__SHELL FRAGMENT WIDE RIGHT FEMUR P.O. SCAR SYMPTOMATIC.__

The monthly payments pursuant to this award will continue during the period in which you are __10%__ disabled subject to the general conditions mentioned on the reverse side of this communication to which your attention is directed. Upon the happening of any of the contingencies mentioned the Veterans Administration should be notified promptly.

It has been determined that service connection is not shown for the following conditions __NONE__

If you are dissatisfied with the findings of the Veterans Administration or the amount of this award it is your privilege to enter an appeal therefrom within 1 year from the date of this communication. Such appeal should be submitted to this office for certification to the Board of Veterans' Appeals, Washington 25, D. C.

If you should change your present address the Veterans Administration must be immediately notified.

All future communications with reference to this case should be addressed to this office and must bear the file number C __-5,851,945__ as well as your full name and complete rank and organization.

Encl:
Notice of Entitlement to Treatment.
Form..... 106.
Form .... 1900.

W. F. GREENE, Adjudication Officer

215 West 24th St., New York 11, N.Y.
(SEE OTHER SIDE)   Veterans Administration.

Disability award of $11.50 a month for wounds suffered in Market-Garden combat action in Holland in 1944 (left).

Form 260 a

APPLICATION FOR APPOINTMENT
Courier
AS XXXXXX IN THE
FOREIGN SERVICE OF THE UNITED STATES

All questions must be answered fully

Date of application *April 17 1946*

Handed in
Acknowledged
Field applican
Carded
Indexed
Investigated
Action

The HONORABLE
THE SECRETARY OF STATE,
Washington, D.C.
SIR:
I hereby apply for appointment as a XXXX Courier in the Foreign Service to serve in an American Mission or Consulate.

Respectfully,

Hugh Francis Redmond
(Sign, using customary Christian name, not merely initials)

1. (a) Name in full: *Hugh Francis Redmond*
(b) Permanent address: *65 Belmont Ave, Yonkers, N.Y.*
(c) Temporary address (if any):
(d) Telephone number (if living in Washington or vicinity):
(e) State of which you are legal resident: *New York* Length of residence: *26 yrs*
2. Place and date of birth: *Yonkers* *N.Y.* *30* *Oct* *1919*
(City or town) (State) (Day) (Month) (Year)
3. Marital status: *Single* Dependents: *none*
(a) Name of husband (or wife):
(b) Place and date of birth of husband (or wife):
(City or town) (State) (Day) (Month) (Year)
(c) Nationality of husband (or wife):
(d) Is your husband now in Army or Navy?
4. (a) Name of father: *Hugh Redmond Sr* Nationality: *Amer.*
(b) Place and date of birth of father: *Yonkers, N.Y.* *May 9 1884*
(c) Permanent address of father: *65 Belmont Ave, Yonkers*
5. (a) Maiden name of mother: *Ruth Murphy* Nationality: *Amer.*
(b) Place and date of birth of mother: *Yonkers, N.Y.* *Oct 2, 1898*
(c) Permanent address of mother: *65 Belmont Ave Yonkers*

19. Give below, in your own handwriting, a description of the experience which you have outlined under item 18, paying particular attention to any experience which, in your opinion, qualifies you for the position for which this application is filed. Begin your description of experience in each separate position on a new line, numbering each description to correspond with the number of the section in which the position is listed under item 18.

1 *I was a parachutist for the entire time in service which should qualify me as far as physical condition and adaptability are concerned. Know morse code and army field radios plus code clerk work. Converters, strips, pre-arranged etc. In a series of tests taken at New York University was graded 96th percentile.*

20. Have you ever been arrested for anything other than minor traffic violations? *no*. If so, give details on a separate sheet.
21. The applicant transmits an unmounted photograph, taken in 194_6_, with his name written thereon, and a birth certificate.
22. What restrictions are there, if any, on your immediate availability for duty in any part of the world? *none*

I do solemnly affirm that the information contained herein is correct to the best of my knowledge and belief; that I do not advocate the overthrow of the Government of the United States by force or violence; that I am not a member of any political party or organization that advocates the overthrow of the Government of the United States by force or violence.

Hugh F Redmond
(Name of usually written and which will be used as official signature)

Application for appointment to the OSS, later the CIA, dated April 17, 1946. Four months later, he was on his way to China.

Form 6569
TREASURY DEPARTMENT
Treasurer, U. S.—Accounting Division
(Revised)

(Note.—The grantor's Christian name, additional initials, if any, and surname should be used in the execution of the power of attorney.)

POWER OF ATTORNEY BY INDIVIDUAL FOR THE COLLECTION OF CHECKS DRAWN ON THE TREASURER OF THE UNITED STATES

Know all Men by these Presents:

That the undersigned, _____ **Hugh F. Redmond** _____, of

65 Belmont Ave., Yonkers, New York _____, does hereby appoint _____
(Post-office address)

Mrs. Ruth Redmond _____, of _____ **65 Belmont Ave., Yonkers, New York**
(Post-office address)

as his attorney to receive, endorse, and collect checks payable to the order of the undersigned, drawn on

the Treasurer of the United States, for whatever account, _____

(See footnote)

and to give full discharge for same, granting to said attorney full power of substitution and revocation, hereby ratifying and confirming all that said attorney, or his substitute, shall lawfully do or cause to be done by virtue hereof.

WITNESS the signature and seal of the undersigned, this _____ 2nd _____ day

of _____ July _____, 1946

_____ Hugh F. Redmond [SEAL]
(Signature of grantor)

Personally appeared before me the above-named _____ Hugh F. Redmond _____
known or proved to me to be the same person who executed the foregoing instrument, and acknowledged to me that he executed the same as his free act and deed.

WITNESS my signature, official designation, and seal.

[IMPRESS SEAL HERE]

_____ Evelyn K. Hall
(Signature of attesting officer)

_____ Notary Public
(Official designation)

Dated at _____ Wash., D. C., this _____ 2nd _____ day of _____ July _____, 1946

My commission expires _____ My Commission Expires 8/13/47 _____, 194_

IMPORTANT.—Do not execute this instrument without first reading the instructions on the reverse side hereof. Exact compliance with these instructions will avoid complications.

Note.—If desired, the words "whatever account" may be stricken out and the space used to insert a description of the particular check or checks involved.
16—16605

July 1946 Power of Attorney allowing Mrs. Redmond to cash her son's U.S. Treasury checks for CIA duties (left).

One of the early Congressional letters indicating U.S. officials' concern about standing up to the Communist Chinese on Redmond's behalf (right).

RALPH W. GWINN
27TH DIST., NEW YORK

WASHINGTON ADDRESS:
ROOM 541,
OLD HOUSE OFFICE BUILDING

COMMITTEE:
EDUCATION AND LABOR

DISTRICT OFFICE:
POST OFFICE BUILDING
YONKERS, NEW YORK

Congress of the United States
House of Representatives
Washington, D. C.

January 3, 1955

Mrs. Ruth Redmond
8 Floral Lane
Yonkers, N. Y.

Dear Mrs. Redmond:

I talked with Assistant Secretary of State Morton as well as with Allyn C. Donaldson, Director, Office of Special Consular Services with reference to Hugh. They have had one conference with the Reds regarding your son's release and they expect to have more. The encouraging thing is that conversations have not been cut off.

The State Department fears that if the United States brings economic pressure or threats it will unite the Chinese behind the Reds all the more. They want to prod us into violence. Let us hope for better word soon.

Sincerely yours,
Ralph W. Gwinn

G/s

DEPARTMENT OF STATE
WASHINGTON

August 2 6, 1959

Dear Mrs. Redmond:

The American Red Cross has informed us that following representations by them, the Chinese Communist Red Cross has finally responded to complaints about the slowness and delays in the forwarding of the prisoners' letters to their families. In a cable to General Gruenther, the Chinese Communist Red Cross announced that henceforth they would affix airmail postage to the prisoners' letters.

This is a considerable retreat on the part of the Communists from their previous stand, and I would be extremely interested to know how effective the new arrangement is. It would be greatly appreciated if you would notify the Department the next time you receive mail from your son giving us the dates of writing, posting and receipt by you.

Sincerely yours,

Edwin W. Martin

Edwin W. Martin
Director for Chinese Affairs

Mrs. Ruth Redmond,
43 Argyle Terrace,
Yonkers, New York.

A 1959 letter from the State Department indicating the Chinese Red Cross was responding to a change in mail privileges for Redmond.

Two views of the Ward Road Prison in China as it looks today.

Dear Mother,   Feb. 7, 1964

Another month, another letter to let you
know I am well and wish you all are the
same.

On the 28th of January, your letters #47, 48
arrived. One of which was written on Xmas
day. So you had a nice white Xmas, that's
really fine. Christmas without snow seems
out of season. Of course there wasn't any
snow here. It rarely snows in Shanghai.
If you haven't already sent some Xmas
snapshots, don't forget to do so.

Have you finally made up your mind
about retiring at the end of this school
year?

Your food packages came on the third.
Last month on the 6th, the two packages
of books you mailed in October arrived.
The November packages haven't come yet.

The "Sports" magazine you send by
mail doesn't come anymore. Only the
first four copies for 1963 came.
So it isn't a question of them being
lost in the mail. They couldn't go
astray that consistently. Please check
and see if it is still being sent.
The "National Geographic" also comes
rather erratically although it is
sent by first class mail.

I received eight copies for 1963.
The seven copies from January through
July, and the October issue. The other
copies didn't come.

I sampled the rice you sent. But I
must say it is not as good as regular
rice. It is also long grain rice which
is not as good as egg-shaped rice.
Do not send anymore, I only wanted
to satisfy my curiosity. The oatmeal
is quite good, so continue to send it.

Say hello to friends for me. Don't
forget to buy icecream for the children.

                    As ever,
                    Hugh

Dear Mother,   Dec. 4, 1965

Merry Christmas to you and the Baylies! And a Happy New Year too! I suppose that you will spend the day at Ruthie's place. I hope that the children will find what they were wishing for under the tree, and that there will be a little something for them from me under the tree too. Little Ruthie is the only one young enough to still believe in Santa Claus, although if she is as clever as you say she is, she may already know better.

There was an article in the Chinese paper last month about a power failure that affected the northeastern states including New York. Was Yonkers blacked out too? What was the reason for such a large scale power failure? I didn't think that the whole area was dependent on only one source of power. Today's paper contained an item about a power failure in Texas and New Mexico also.

About a week after I wrote the Nov. letter I received two packages of books mailed in August. Your letter # 133 mailed the 6th of October was given to me at the same time.

Please write the list of contents on the reverse side of the wrapper on the packages of books as they no longer come in the boxes as before.

Two food packages came yesterday. (containing long underwear). In the future please do not send canned fruit, instead send wheat crackers or cookies. — such as graham crackers or Social Teas. Also discontinue sending marsh mallow cookies, there is no body to them, — like eating air.

I hope that you have a very pleasant Christmas and get around to see friends during the holidays. When you do, be sure to give my best wishes to everyone.

A special Merry Christmas to you and the Baylies,

                    Love,
                    Hugh

Ruth Redmond returns home after a trip to China to see her son Hugh in Ward Road Prison, Shanghai. (Michael Cipriani photo)

Ruth Redmond with committee to Free Hugh Redmond. Attorney Sol Friedman is in the back row, center. (Michael Cipriani photo)

Bustling Shanghai of today along the famed Bund and the dock of Shanghai along the Huanspu River where Redmond was taken prisoner in 1951.

Entrance to Oakland Cemetery gravesite area (page left) where Hugh Redmond is buried. His headstone carries the words "His Country Above All Else" engraved in the stone. (Author's photo)

Last known photo of Redmond, taken by his mother during her 1962 visit at Ward Road Prison, Shanghai. (AP wirephoto)

Chapter 7

The Sixth of June Along The Douve

More than two hundred thousand men, more than thirteen thousand paratroopers, more than five thousand ships waited for the word, the nod of the head, the official "go" of a balding fifty three year old American general who had been born in Denison, Texas and grew up in Abilene, Kansas. All across England, throughout the continent of Europe, across America, expectations increased that the Great Crusade, Operation Overlord, the massive invasion of Europe, would soon be on. Dwight David Eisenhower, who had won his appointment as Supreme Commander in December, 1943 from President Roosevelt on the basis of his military knowledge and skills, huddled with his aides in London's Southwick House. There were German strengths and weaknesses to be considered, tides and weather, men and morale, as the decisions neared. There was even the problem of politics, as Churchill had promised Stalin the second front would be opened in May to take the pressure off the Russians in the East. Now it was June.

The men who would come by air and sea to France were collected in marshaling areas all over the southern coast of England. They were finely tuned, ready, determined, courageous, confident in their youth and motivated by their mission. They knew they must cross the English Channel. They would fight, some would die, but they would push the Germans back, out of France, out of Belgium and Holland, across the Rhone and the Rhine, back into the heart of Germany, to defeat and surrender, a total capitulation before the war could be won. Then they could go home.

"I don't think we were philosophical about the war," says Dick Falvey as he recalls the days he sat ready, restlessly waiting in England. "We never really talked about what it all meant. We knew the good guys from the bad guys. We just kept repeating our motto, 'Home alive in '45.'"

Eisenhower and his staff had made the decision. The invasion would begin in the early hours of Monday, June 5th. The first wave of ships would slip quickly and unobtrusively out to sea on June 4th. There would be a chance to turn back if the weather turned worse.

At 4:30 Sunday morning, June 4th, Eisenhower was to meet again with his aides.

At the marshaling areas the men slept. They were to be awakened at 5:30 in the morning. They completed last minute preparations. Time weighed heavy on their hands. They had been caged behind fences for nearly a week for reasons of security.

Many men attended church services and made their peace with God. "Church services had a lot more men than usual, but not what you would expect from a group about to start an invasion, which is something I really couldn't figure out," reported Lieutenant Richard Winters.

There were some strange last minute happenings — small events remembered through the years.

Captain Arthur B. Lunin, assistant surgeon for the 3rd Battalion of the 501st, said "I treated General Taylor for an ingrown toenail the day before D-Day. I stuffed some cotton under it and told him if I did more I couldn't be sure if he could be with us, and we wanted him."

Major Allen "Pinky" Ginder received a letter from his wife while waiting in the marshaling area. She asked if he had changed his beneficiary on his GI insurance. His own father had been killed as an officer in World War I and had failed to alter his policy in favor of his young wife.

Lieutenant Sumpter Blackmon received a letter with a picture of his wife and newborn son. He showed it to Lieutenant Colonel Harry Kinnard. "Blackie, you've really got something to fight for there," Kinnard said.

After breakfast, expecting to go later that evening, the troops of the

506th were each issued ten dollars in crisp new French money. It had only been minted recently for the invasion.

It was not a gift. It was paid to each man as part of his monthly salary and had to be signed for after waiting in long lines.

The training had all been completed. Now the men simply waited for the word to go. They concentrated on cleaning their weapons, preparing their equipment, reviewing procedures. There was time to kill so they played cards, shot dice, read books, wrote letters home to their loved ones. The clock moved slowly. Time was more of an enemy now than the Germans were.

Many of the men from the 3rd Battalion of the 506th, including Robert Webb, Jim Bradley, Ray Calendrella and Hugh Redmond attended a movie quickly set up on a screen in a huge hanger. PFC Clair Mathiason, in George Koskimaki's splendid book *D-Day with the Screaming Eagles,* describes what happened next.

"We were treated to a show. It was a war movie. It was about the bombing of some enemy city. It was a tense moment in the movie when the incident occurred. The bombs were dropping at the time in the movie and there was a terrible hissing noise in the hangar. Something came crashing down at the back of the darkened area. It caused a commotion and everyone immediately thought there was a real bombing going on and in one great movement everyone started for the doors. Chairs were knocked over. By the time everyone was outside and realized there was no attack, we had suffered the first casualties of the war. There were a couple of boys hurt in the mad rush to get out and as I remember two had broken legs. It turned out a fire extinguisher hanging at the back of the room had been knocked down and set off. I remember the verbal going-over we got from Colonel Wolverton for being so easily shaken up, and how he wondered what we would be like under fire."

The rest of that afternoon was spent checking last minute details. Many men busied themselves carefully sewing on small American flags five inches by three inches to their right sleeves. Others wrote letters home. Some had their hair cut off. A few exchanged addresses with their buddies and asked them to visit parents or wives if they didn't make it.

The weather charts were studied thoroughly by Eisenhower and his staff in the early hours of June 5th. The signs were encouraging. The invasion was now on schedule. It was too late to turn back again. The ships were moving. The entire operation had begun. The point of no return had been passed. Sometime that Monday, as described by David Howarth in *D Day*, Eisenhower drafted an announcement without telling anyone. He put it in his pocket in case it was needed. He found it again, six weeks later and showed to his naval aide, who kept it as a souvenir. The Commanding General had written, "Our landings in the Cherbourg-Havre area have failed to gain a satisfactory foothold and I have withdrawn the troops. My decision to attack at this time and place was based on the best information available. The troops, the Air Force and the Navy did all that bravery and devotion to duty could do. If any blame or fault is attached to the event it is mine alone."

At 5:30 that evening, the fifth of June, the men of the 506th sat down to their final meal before the invasion of Europe. They ate steak, green peas, mashed potatoes, white bread, ice cream and coffee. "Not a bad last meal for condemned men," Hugh Redmond said to Dick Falvey. They went back to their assembly areas. Many blackened their faces with charcoal. Redmond lit up a cigarette and said, "I'll pass," when a buddy asked if he wanted charcoal. He checked the straps of his radio hanging from a bag on his left leg.

The men were at the staging areas now. Planes were everywhere. They sat in small groups waiting for instructions to board. The young pilots, their scarves blowing in the breeze, walked up and down the runway. Many of the troops slept. Some of them read letters tucked in their pockets.

Soon there was a bustle of excitement through the ranks. Somebody whispered "Ike is here," and all the men began leaping to their feet to see the Supreme Commander at the air field, talking with some officers. In a few minutes he walked with his aide from the group of officers toward the fighting men. He came to talk to individual groups of soldiers, asking them questions, shaking hands and chatting easily with them. One soldier asked Ike to sign his "short-snorter," an autographed dollar bill. Another asked if he could pose for a picture. Eisenhower seemed genuinely interested in the background of each man and deeply concerned with each man's welfare.

"Where are you from, son?" Eisenhower asked one young soldier.

"Texas. sir. Waco, Texas."

"That's some fine ranch country," the general said. "I was born in Texas. I know that area well. Good luck, son."

Then he walked to another group, chatted with those men and finally walked over to one young soldier, who could hardly have been more than seventeen years old.

"What do you do, son?"

"Ammunition bearer, sir."

"Where is your home?"

"Pennsylvania, sir."

"Did you get those shoulders working in a coal mine?"

"Yes, sir."

"Good luck to you tonight, soldier."

Corporal Kermit R. Latta recalled the scene vividly. "I was struck by the terrific burden of decision and responsibility on his face," wrote Corporal Latta.

One of the most famous photos of World War II shows General Eisenhower, his hands stuffed in his pants pockets, his face warm and animated, his eyes concentrating on the man he is talking to, interviewing a paratrooper with head shaved, face blackened, and helmet camouflaged, minutes before the planes took off for Normandy.

For each man, as the seconds ticked off, there was his own private memory of this historic evening. Staff Sergeant Jerry McCullough remembered a last minute talk by Colonel Wolverton, who had trained 3rd Battalion from the start at Camp Toccoa. Now Colonel Wolverton stood on a small mound of earth, facing these men in southern England.

"Men, I am not a religious man," Colonel Wolverton began, "and I don't know your feelings in this matter, but I am going to ask you to pray with me for the success of the mission before us. And while we pray, let us get down on our knees and not look down but up with faces raised to the sky.

"God All Mighty, in a few short hours we will be in battle with the enemy. We do not join battle afraid. We do not ask favors or indulgence but ask that if You will, use us as Your instruments for the right and an aid in returning peace to the world.

"We do not know or seek what our fate will be. We ask only this, that if die we must, that we die as men would die, without complaining, without pleading and safe in the feeling that we have done our best for what we believe was right.

"Oh Lord, protect our loved ones and be near us in the fire ahead and with us now as we each pray to you."

There was silence for a few moments, and then Colonel Wolverton, in his booming West Point-trained voice, called, "Move out."

The men of the 506th were moving on to war.

The men moved to their planes and began boarding as they had been trained to do. They had been through this so many times before that it was all done calmly, in an orderly fashion, as a matter of course, as it always had been done before. There were to be twenty men lined up in single file at jump time, a stick of twenty in paratrooper parlance, with four crew members on the plane. The crew chief would assist the troopers with the plane door at the time of the drop.

Redmond looked out and could see the British airfield workers standing in the shadows as the planes made ready to take off. Many stood at attention and saluted. Others gave the thumbs-up sign of Churchill's famed V for Victory sign. There were tears in their eyes.

It was 10:45. The engines kicked on. The sound seemed incredibly loud. Close. Ominous. Frightening. At one minute before eleven on June 5, 1944, the plane roared forward, raced down the runway, lifted off smoothly and headed east toward France.

Redmond closed his eyes and tried to sleep. His mouth was dry. His legs felt cold and weak. His stomach seemed empty. He licked his lips. He reached into his musette bag with his right hand and pulled out a pack of cigarettes. He lit one up, took a deep drag and leaned back. It made him feel a little more relaxed.

More than five hundred planes from fifty separate air fields in England, carrying more than six thousand men of the 101st Airborne Division were now moving in waves over France. They flew in carefully charted routes, some actually passing over their drop zones, proceeding further west in a coordinated attempt to disguise their true targets, before turning back east and throttling down to unload their young men into the night.

Some of the men sat with eyes closed against the back of the planes. Some smoked cigarettes. Many just stared straight ahead as their minds filled with thoughts of home and family. There were a few who joked and laughed as the planes flew swiftly across the French countryside. Redmond looked at his watch. He knew the drop zone would be approaching soon. He was ready. He awaited instructions, thinking of how he would act, what he must do, how he would maintain himself if he were cut off from his squad.

The signal came. A red light flashed in the plane. The jumpmaster leaped up and yelled, "Stand up and hook up." Men attached their chutes to the static line. One man said, "I wish the boys in the office could see me now." They checked each other's lines. They tugged at their equipment to see that all was in proper order. The jumpmaster yelled, "Is everybody happy?" The men answered loudly as one, "YES!" The door of the plane was pulled open. The flak came closer. The sky was clear. The moon was bright. Tracers raced near them. A green light flashed. "GO!" and the first man was out, yelling, "Bill Lee," in honor of their former commander. The second man in the stick was out the door. The third. The fourth. The plane seemed to sway as flak exploded everywhere. Now the fifth, the sixth and the seventh. Now Hugh Francis Redmond was at the door, shouting "Bill Lee!" and falling from seven hundred feet, concentrating on keeping his chin tightly tucked into his chest, holding his legs together to avoid the violent thrust at his groin, looking up quickly for an instant to see his beautiful camouflage colored parachute fully extended, feeling the wind pulling at him, looking down, trying hard to recognize any contour of the earth he had seen so many times before on the maps, seeing tracers all around him, and watching other troops already nearing the ground, finally seeing the Douve River coming up fast at him.

Soldiers of the German 709th Infantry Division, waiting more than a year for the invasion, were asleep in the farms and villages of Normandy. In one of the guard posts a sentry spotted an open parachute, then another, another and another. He cranked his phone madly as he stared open-mouthed at the objects falling from the sky. The phone was answered by a sleepy voice. The sentry shouted, "Amerikaner fallschirmjaeger, Amerikaner fallschirmjaeger, Amerikaner fallschirmjaeger!"

Hugh Redmond, American paratrooper, was in France. The time was 1:54 A.M. on the sixth of June, 1944. This was D-Day.

Chapter 8

Hero With The 506th Infantry

All of the men in Hugh Redmond's stick fell on the west side of the Douve River. Redmond was the only man in twenty to fall on the east side of the river. It saved his life.

"He told me later he had stumbled coming out of the door," said Dick Falvey. "The guy in front of him had slowed up. Redmond caught his boot on the other guy's heel."

The west side of the river was heavily fortified by German troops. German fields of fire caught most of the men, even before they could get out of their harnesses. Two drowned in the river. One was shot and killed as he stood up near the river's edge to study his map. Another died when he crashed into a stone building.

There was confusion everywhere. The Germans weren't sure what was happening. They had no way of knowing if the Amerikaner fallschir-mjaeger were the forerunners of a massive invasion of troops by sea, or merely a reconnaissance group sent by air to gain information, as the British often did. The Americans were just as confused. They had been dropped all over Normandy — some as far as twenty miles from assigned drop zones. Some fell in the middle of towns, on roofs of houses, on church steeples, through farm houses, into barns, in the middle of fields, against hedgerows, in soft piles of cow dung.

Parachute troops are independent warriors. They must be. They jump alone. In some cases, it would be minutes, even hours or days, before they would march up to a friendly face. The experiences of no two troops on that moonlit night in France were exactly the same. Every man was on his own coming down, generals and privates alike, until they could join together in some cohesive units.

General Maxwell Taylor landed in a field of cows. He unharnessed his parachute, looked around, spotted a rifleman unharnessing nearby and started this part of his war in Europe with one man under his command.

Lieutenant Colonel Robert Wolverton, battalion commander of the 3rd battalion of the 506th, was in the battalion's lead plane as he jumped near drop zone D.

"I was in the same plane as Colonel Wolverton," said Bill Pauli, then a message center chief for Wolverton's battalion. "I remember him standing near the door, grumbling because he knew we were way off our drop zones. We all jumped and it was a shock to me to see how light it was, with a bright moon and enemy flares lighting up the sky."

The drop was supposed to be over open farm land. It turned out to be over heavy hedgerow country with wooded areas all around them. Colonel Wolverton was heading toward a wooded area. He could not maneuver his parachute away and the chute caught in a tree. Wolverton was imprisoned in its branches. At daybreak he was found still hanging in the tree, shot dead with two bullet holes in his head.

Ray Calendrella was in the same plane with Wolverton and Pauli.

"I didn't see Colonel Wolverton after we dropped. I had no idea what had happened to him. Nobody did. When I landed, I found myself in a large field. I was alone. Then I heard the click of a cricket. I answered back and joined up with a couple of other guys. Soon there were seven or eight of us. At daybreak a few more guys joined us. There were Germans all around us. We survived a few fire fights and kept moving in the direction of the bridges. At night we rested against a hedgerow. We were ambushed. Four of the guys were killed and the rest of us scattered again."

Calendrella and three others moved through the night of June sixth after hiding out all day. On the afternoon of the seventh, they ran into more German soldiers.

"Three more of our guys were killed. I had just given first aid to one of them and baptized him before he died. I looked up and there were nine or ten German soldiers holding their guns on me."

Calendrella was captured and help prisoner for eighty three days. He was being held temporarily in a farmhouse near Charlons-sur-Marne where a number of American prisoners awaited transportation to camps back in Germany.

"A fellow from another division and I had inspected the farmhouse. We discovered it had a small attic. We squeezed ourselves through a narrow trap door and hid in the space between the ceiling and the roof. The Germans came for us, made their count, discovered two of us missing and began searching. They banged on the ceiling with their weapons but never found the door. They finally moved out without us. We escaped and got back to our own lines. I rejoined the 506th for the rest of the war," Calendrella said.

Bill Pauli had jumped out of the same plane with Wolverton and Calendrella. Staff sergeant Pauli was vital to the success of the drop as message center chief. As it turned out with so many paratroopers on D Day, Pauli was not dropped when he was supposed to be and never could perform his assigned task. He was injured in the jump. There are memories of how tracers streaked the skies, whistling and cracking against the metal of the nearby planes as the young man from Montana struggled to escape.

"I felt like a sitting duck," he said. "I let my chute oscillate to make a more difficult target. I landed on the ground with great shock and pain. I found I could not move my legs and I had excruciating pain in my lower back. Finally I got out of my chute and tried to orient myself. It sounded like a mill pond with all those mechanical crickets. One of my runners was the first man I saw. His name was John Rinehart — he was a young replacement who had joined us in England. I told him to take it easy until things quieted down, but he took off running and was cut down by a machine gun at the first hedgerow. A medic came by a short time later but could not help me as I had no open wounds."

The pain grew more intense as Pauli lay, unable to move, in an open field. The firing was heavy all around him. He could hear small fire fights behind his position. Finally he decided to cover himself with his parachute, hoping to be picked up later by friendly troops. He passed out from the intense pain in his broken left pelvis.

"As daylight arrived, I awoke when I felt my chute being pulled off me. I looked up to see two Germans who in turn stripped me of my watch, cigarettes, billfold and weapon. They picked me up and took me to St. Come-du-Mont. Feeling low in spirits, I was surprised to see how many comrades-in-arms were there ahead of me. The Germans had only a field aid station, so they put me in a barn with other 101st men, and left us."

Two days later the Americans captured St. Come-du-Mont. Pauli was shipped back to England, recovered in a hospital during the summer of 1944, and rejoined his outfit in September, in time for the jump into Holland.

"I was a platoon sergeant by December," he said. "I was on leave in Paris. One afternoon the MPs came driving through. Wherever they saw soldiers they shouted, 'Any Screaming Eagles here?'. I jumped up and got into a jeep with them. They drove us all the way to Bastogne in Belgium. Our Division had been encircled. The Battle of the Bulge was on. I had to wait several days before a hole opened in the German lines and we could rush through, so I could rejoin my Division."

One of the main obstacles for the paratroopers of the 101st that night was water. Many men lost their lives in rivers, ponds and streams, loaded down with equipment and unable to move. They drowned in water only three or four feet deep as they slipped and stumbled, unable to get up.

"I had no trouble seeing that night," remembers Robert Webb. "The tracers did a good job of lighting up the sky. I was loaded down with communications equipment — a radio, extra batteries, a leg pack filled with everything we needed. I carried a carbine. I must have weighed over three hundred pounds as I jumped."

Webb floated down through enemy fire, tried to pick out landmarks, and saw his chute oscillating dangerously close to the Douve River.

"I pulled and tugged but couldn't get away from the water. I splashed right in. The Germans were firing twenty millimeter guns at me. The water was about up to my neck. I fell a couple of times and couldn't move up the river bank. I saw a branch and reached for it. I dropped my carbine and it floated away. I was left with a 45 caliber pistol and a trench knife to fight the whole German army. I grabbed at the branch and was able to hold on for a while. Then I began losing my grip. I was sure I would drown."

As Webb was about to fall backward into the water — with his strength ebbing and his equipment heavily soaked, he realized he would never be able to reach level ground. He saw a hand reaching for him.

"I looked up and it was another paratrooper. I don't know his name to this day. He got on his belly at the water's edge and pulled me out. I owe him my life," Webb said.

Webb, who had left his quiet job as a clerk in Woolworth's to join the paratroopers, lay on the ground above the river and rested. Suddenly he saw a lone German solder walking toward them, his rifle drawn. He pulled his pistol from his belt, rolled over and killed the German soldier with one shot to the head.

"After that I was able to join up with the other guys. I stayed with the 101st through the rest of the war, into Germany. I came home in September of 1945 and have been here in Houston every since," Webb said.

Jim Bradley, the banker from California, remembers the night of June fourth in England almost as much as the night of June fifth over France.

"The first night we were to go I felt uneasy, nervous, unsure of myself. I can't explain why. I just wasn't ready. Then the drop was postponed for twenty four hours. The next night I was fine — felt confident, prepared, quite comfortable about the whole thing. I never thought about getting killed. Being so young, it was just something that never entered my mind."

Bradley was number five in a sixteen man stick. His jump was smooth. He landed easily in an open field just outside St. Come-du-Mont under heavy mortar fire.

"I was with a medic and two sergeants from a rifle company," he remembers. "I knew our assembly area was north toward the river. I got out a flashlight and looked at my map. The medic went off to look for a road. He popped into the bushes, crept down the hill and disappeared. In a few minutes he was back. The two other guys had taken off in another direction."

Farms in the Normandy countryside were small. Each farmer separated his farm from his neighbor's by heavily grown bushes known as hedgerows. These hedgerows played a vital part of that evening's maneuvers. Many men lost their lives in the hedgerows — ambushed by Germans they couldn't see on the other side. Many Germans suffered a similar fate at the hands of the Americans.

"We moved north toward the next hedgerow," says Bradley. "Those hedgerows were about six feet tall. You could walk almost without being seen. Some of them were bordered by stone walls. Suddenly Kraut machine guns fired on us and we ran toward another hedgerow. The firing continued. I was hit."

Bradley was alone now. He leaned against the hedgerow and jammed another clip into his rifle.

"I remember thinking, 'This is where I fight my war.' I just lay still. In a few hours, it was dawn. A German patrol came walking down the road near me. I held my breath. The point of the patrol walked by me. Then the first man went by. The second stuck his weapon into the hedgerow and spotted me. I stood up, they took my weapon, marched me back and held me in a barn with other prisoners. They treated my wound and shipped me deeper into France, later moved me to Belgium and finally into Germany. I was freed in May of 1945."

Bradley spent nearly eleven months as a prisoner of war.

"We threw them a few curves while I was there. We had all read the rules. We started saluting their officers, observing strict military procedure, operating with tight discipline. It surprised them that we could be such good soldiers. I think it helped us survive," Bradley said.

Dick Falvey remembers how quickly his priorities changed when he landed in Normandy that night.

"I had all my pockets filled with candy. As soon as I hit the ground I realized I was in the wrong place. Nothing looked the way it was supposed to look from the maps," he said.

The fire was heavy from German small arms on the ground. Several planes exploded over Falvey's head, sending debris throughout the area.

"My only thought was about being captured. I had all the radio code books in my pocket. I quickly pulled out my knife and began digging a hole in the ground. I got out the books, tore them into small pieces and buried them in several different places. I was concerned about the Germans winning the war because if they captured me and my codes, they would have understood all our transmissions."

Falvey also got rid of much of his extra equipment, then moved out to find another paratrooper.

"The first guy I saw was Joe Slesarczyk. He was a pigeonnaire. I gave him one snap of the cricket and he gave me two snaps. Two days later, Joe was killed in a fire fight."

After Falvey and Slesarczyk made contact, other troops joined them. Soon there were about twenty men together. They found a farm house and walked carefully toward it.

"One of our guys spoke French," said Falvey. "He went inside and asked where the hell we were. The Frenchmen couldn't understand that we had come from the sky. He thought we were the invasion troops who had come from the sea. He finally was able to help us out and we left to move toward our assembly area. We gave him one of the crickets for a souvenir. I bet there are Frenchmen all over that country who still have those crickets, even now. French women, too. I don't know of anyone who brought his cricket back home. I do know of a few guys who brought their French girls back home, though."

Hugh Redmond had landed more than a mile and a half east and south of the Douve River in cold swampy marshlands. Water soaked into his boots on contact. He lay still for an instant, making sure he was all in one piece. Then he rolled over, pulled off one strap of his parachute harness, then the other, and got up on one knee. He looked around quickly and saw no enemy troops. He could hear the sound of small arms fire off in the distance to his left and could see a huge trail of smoke billowing from the sky. He pulled his map from his left breast pocket and his compass from his right pocket. He reasoned that he had to be on the east side

. of the river, since he had seen the water behind him when he jumped. He decided that he must be in the marsh land north of Carentan and some three to three and a half miles from his assigned drop zone D.

Redmond knew he had to make his way quickly to the Douve River bridges. The mission of the 3rd battalion was to seize and hold the two wooden bridges across the Douve, to prevent German reinforcements from crossing first and hitting the landing force that would be arriving at Utah Beach in some four and a half hours. Redmond knew his presence was vital to the mission. He was a trained radio operator and had been promoted to Corporal and wire chief in his platoon just before the invasion. He was skilled in telephone and telegraph communications, codes and transmissions. He had scored high marks in all his Army exams on sending and receiving Morse code. He could transmit rapidly and accurately under stressful conditions.

He took one last look around the area, saw no one else, felt for the cricket in his pocket and started running north. Loaded down with radio equipment and wet boots, he still managed to move quickly through the soggy marsh lands. He was running hard now in his own personal Olympics. In a few minutes he reached high ground, and lay still at the top of a small incline, studying the open fields before him. He could see a hedgerow well in front of him. There were a few large trees at the end of the hedgerow.

Then he saw two German soldiers, rifles drawn, moving toward him less than fifty yards away.

The land was open. There was no cover, no place to hide, no way of avoiding a confrontation. He pulled himself up to the crest of the small incline, took a deep breath and waited. He could hear their voices now and make out their faces. He had to move quickly or he would be dead. He exploded from the mound of earth, firing quick bursts from his carbine, seeing one of the Germans fall backward, watching the other try to turn back, seeing him fall, all in a brilliant flash of light. Then all was quiet. He knelt on the hill for an instant, then began running fast, moving past the fallen bodies without a glance, crossing the field as if it were a hard dirt track.

He was nearing the hedgerow now from the south and crept slowly toward it. He reached the brush, poked his weapon through the end of the opening and saw the Douve River. He also saw more than a half dozen paratroopers digging in at the east bank of the river. He pulled out his cricket, clicked once as he moved closer, received two clicks in return, then stood up.

It was 4:30 A.M.

Redmond joined up with Robert Webb and others of headquarters company, 3rd battalion of the 506th at the bridges under the command of Colonel Charles Shottle.

Only one hundred and seventeen men out of a battalion of more than eight hundred men made it to the bridges across the Douve River. Since no word had reached Allied headquarters that the bridges were in American hands, and since their demolition was considered essential to the security of the troops soon to be advancing inland from Utah Beach, the Air Corps had been ordered to blow up the bridges. The men of the 506th moved away as the planes made their first strike.

"I remember after everything settled down and we told each other how we made it to the bridges," says Robert Webb, "how proud Hugh Redmond was. He knew he was part of something big. He knew he had really done his job well against some damn heavy odds."

There was time to relax now, to laugh a little, to tell each other how well they had performed in their first combat experience. They complimented each other on surviving. Their lives would never again be quite the same.

"We sat around that night, thinking about what we had been through," says Webb, "considering how we had survived when so many of our buddies hadn't. Some of the guys started talking about celebrating the event together every year."

Redmond turned to Webb and said, "Let's form a club. We'll call ourselves the 1:54 Club for our jump time. We'll meet once a year in a hotel in the middle of the country — say in Kansas City."

Said Webb, "And we'll make our theme song *Home Alive in '45, We're Home Alive In '45.*"

The sun was breaking through along the coast of France. It was 6:30 A.M. and the American paratroopers, who had been in France some five hours, rested near the Douve River. They could hear the shelling increase along the shoreline. The first landing craft of the Allied invasion was hitting the beaches. There would still be bitter fighting ahead for the paratroopers as they moved inland with the main infantry forces. More men would be killed, more wounded and maimed, more captured. On June 17th, they would engage in their last battle of the Normandy campaign, be sent back to Carentan to await orders and to be relieved by the 83rd Division on June 20th.

On July 7th, standing atop a German pillbox in a large field outside Cherbourg, General Taylor addressed his battle tested veterans.

"You hit the ground running toward the enemy," the General said. "You have proved the German soldier is no superman. You have beaten him on his own ground and you can beat him on any ground."

On July 10th they boarded LCTs at Utah Beach and were shipped back to England. They had been in France for thirty five days, and most of the troops laughed to themselves when they recalled an impassioned pep talk before the invasion from General Taylor. He had told them they could expect three days of hard fighting, and then they would be withdrawn. General Lee had told them two years before, "You have a rendezvous with destiny." They had kept the faith and proven their mettle.

The cost had been horrendous. Nearly two-thirds of all the men of the 101st Airborne Division who had jumped on D-Day were killed, captured or wounded. Third battalion had suffered heavy losses with more than two hundred of its finest young men left behind in French cemeteries.

Hugh Redmond would think about that all the way back to England.

It would be written later in the scrapbook of the 506th Parachute Infantry Regiment above a list of names of those killed in action:

WE HAVE ONLY DIED IN VAIN IF YOU BELIEVE SO;
YOU MUST DECIDE THE WISDOM OF OUR CHOICE
BY THE WORLD THAT YOU SHALL BUILD UPON
THE HEADSTONES AND THE EVERLASTING
TRUTHS WHICH HAVE YOUR VOICE.

Chapter 9

Market Garden and Beyond

The fame of the 101st Airborne Division spread quickly throughout America. They had gained a great deal of attention for their part in the D Day operation. In Yonkers, the Redmonds awaited a letter from Hugh. The V-Mail came one afternoon.

"It is a beautiful summer day as I write this. We didn't have much chance to see a lot of France," Redmond wrote his parents, "but I do hope we get to Paris the next time we are there. I would like very much to visit the Louvre and see the Eiffel Tower. I am going to London tomorrow and will send you a postcard from there. I am well and hope you all are the same at home."

"Hugh never wrote much about what he saw in the war," says Ruth Boyle. "He simply didn't want to worry my parents. He knew they could read all about the 101st Airborne in the newspapers. He didn't want them concerned for him. He was always very kind that way."

England was especially lovely that summer, the hills rich and green, the skies clear and bright, the people cheerful, knowing now that the tide of the war had definitely turned toward the Allies and that the war they had fought for five years would soon be reaching its climactic stage.

The return to Ramsbury had been a joyous occasion for the men of the 506th. The warm beer had never tasted as good, the girls had never been more friendly, the grass had never looked as green. New uniforms were issued and the entire regiment received a seven day furlough. When they returned there were ceremonies honoring their fallen comrades. There were medals pinned on their special heroes. Then one afternoon the entire division was assembled. General Eisenhower, General Taylor, General McAuliffe and other field grade officers stood at attention with them as the men of the 101st became part of a new organization called the First Allied Airborne. Included in this new organization were both American airborne divisions, the 101st and the 82nd, three American infantry divisions, three British divisions of airborne and infantry and a Polish brigade.

Through late August and early September of 1944 rumors abounded as to the location of the new drop. The men were moved to marshaling areas on three separate occasions but never received the orders to jump. Conditions kept changing. Plans were difficult to formalize. As the days of September cooled and shortened, the men of the 101st talked longingly about a drop in the Pacific. They felt certain that a drop in the exotic South Pacific would help end the war.

On September 16, 1944, Hugh Redmond, Robert Webb, Ray Calendrella, Bill Pauli, Dick Falvey and the other men of the 506th drew ten dollars in Dutch guilders. The drop was now scheduled for Holland. The massive air drop and battle plan had a code name among the high command: MARKET-GARDEN.

The plan had been devised by Eisenhower's deputy, Field Marshall Bernard L. Montgomery. It was divided into two separate actions, a massive parachute jump between the Dutch towns of Eindhoven and Arnhem, designed to capture the road between the two cities and open it for a huge assault through Arnhem and across the Rhine River into Germany. This was coded as the "MARKET" aspect. Then a concentrated ground assault through Holland from the south, sweeping north to join the paratroopers at Arnhem and moving into the industrial Ruhr valley of Germany, into the German manufacturing cities of Essen and Dusseldorf which was the aspect known as "GARDEN." The combined operation was to be coordinated in such force that Germany would be brought to its knees before the end of 1944.

On Sunday morning, September 17, 1944, Hugh Redmond climbed aboard a C-47 and sat down on the aluminum bucket seat. He stared up at the pale green interior of the plane, took a deep breath, stuck a cigarette in his mouth and sat back for the flight to Holland. He felt comfortable, experienced, proud to be part of another drop that might end the war and send him and his pals back home.

"We were veterans by then," Dick Falvey says. "We had gotten some replacements in England. We spent a great deal of our time helping those new replacements get over their initial nervousness."

Soon the starters were turned on and the plane engines belched forth smoke, the motors turned smoothly and the craft moved into line, roaring down the runway now, heading east again, passing over the English countryside, crossing the Channel for the second time. Soon they were moving over France, turning north to head for the drop zones in Holland near the town of Zon.

It was 1:30 P.M. on a clear, sunny Sunday afternoon in Holland.

Now the sky was filling with parachutes, opening one after another, the camouflage seemingly pointless on such a bright afternoon. The first troops hit the ground some sixty miles behind German lines, falling fast, the drop zone surprisingly clear of the enemy. Their only opposition was some small amount of flak fired at the planes from a great distance, the daylight arrival onto dry soft ground a much sweeter sensation than the wet wooded, heavily defended drop zones of D-Day.

The drop was completed slightly north and east of the town of Zon. Unlike Normandy, the entire regiment was assembled, except for a few self-inflicted drop casualties, in a little less than ninety minutes. The paratroopers moved south quickly, toward Eindhoven, reached the Wilhelmina Canal where they found light resistance, then crossed the canal over a small foot bridge after the Germans blew the three major bridge crossings.

At nine o'clock on the morning of September 18, the 3rd battalion of the 506th ran into heavy fire just outside the city limits of Eindhoven. The 2nd battalion was ordered to move west, coming into the city from a flanking position. The tactic worked and at 10:30 P.M. Eindhoven fell to the 506th, the first city in Holland to be liberated. Just to show that the entire operation was not going to be a piece of cake, the Germans bombed the troops at Eindhoven at 8:15 P.M.

On the morning of September 22nd, the entire regiment was ordered to move north up the Eindhoven-Arnhem road, stopping at the town of Uden, some twenty two miles north of Eindhoven and twenty eight miles south of Arnhem. They were to build a defense line there against a German counterattack. Advance elements of 2nd battalion moved into Uden at 9:40 A.M. The bulk of the regiment was still on the road south of Veghel when the Germans suddenly pushed a Panzer tank division across the road from the east and met up with infantry forces from the west, effectively closing the road and trapping the advance party of 2nd battalion at Uden.

The 506th was engaged in the toughest fighting it had experienced in the late afternoon of September 22nd as its commander, Colonel Robert Sink, fought hard to open the road and free his embattled troops in Uden. The men had not seen much fire against armored tanks in Normandy. Now they were seeing far too much. The Germans unloaded with their Panzers, with heavy mortar fire and a driving attack of small arms. In the early evening the possession of the road was still in doubt.

At the outskirts of Veghel the troops of the 506th began squeezing the Germans back. They entered the town in force after some heavy skirmishes and the Germans retreated to the northern side of the town. Some German soldiers were left behind to slow the American advance. They hid inside houses, behind small cars and trucks, at the corners of buildings, at the end of small cobblestone streets. The Allied troops were alert to the short, sharp crack of enemy fire bursting in the streets.

Men from the communications platoon of headquarters company of the 3rd battalion of the 506th, Hugh Redmond among them, moved carefully through the town, bent low, eyes moving quickly from rooftop to rooftop, from house to house, searching out the enemy with the sixth sense of veteran warriors. Suddenly a burst of machine gun fire came from a home to their left. Redmond fired back at the rear window of the small house. He could hear a cry and saw a German soldier fall forward onto a window sill. Then there was quiet again.

Redmond looked down at his left leg. It felt warm. He could see blood oozing through a tear in his pants just below the left calf. He had been hit by machine gun fire which had ricocheted off the cobblestones, bounced up and caught him in the leg. He tried to continue on with his squad. He could only drag his leg. The bleeding increased. He felt the sweat pouring off him, running down his face and under his shirt collar, soaking his neck, back and shoulders.

"Medic," he called out.

In a few minutes Redmond was given a smoke, put in a jeep and driven to a small aid station near Zon. The wound was not serious. He was treated quickly and sent back to join his unit in less than forty eight hours.

The regiment had moved north past Uden into Opheusden by the morning of October 5, 1944. The 363rd German Infantry Division moved on the town with a strong attack at three o'clock in the morning. The 506th held. Two hours later the Germans regrouped and attacked again, this time pushing the paratroopers back inch by bloody inch through heavy artillery fire and then in hand to hand fighting. Third battalion had given ground grudgingly, moving some four hundred yards back in twelve hours. First battalion of the 506th, held in reserve, advanced through the lines of 3rd battalion and recaptured all of the ground lost to the Germans by six o'clock that evening. Fierce artillery fire continued through the night. In the early morning hours of the sixth of October the Germans intensified their artillery and mortar attacks on the soldiers of the 1st and 3rd battalions dug in around the city.

"The fire was intense," remembers Bill Pauli. "We needed help. Our communications were cut off. We needed new wire laid if we were to get help and stay alive."

There was no safe way to lay wire under the intense German barrage. The men seemed resigned to the fact that no reinforcements could be contacted and no aid could be expected. More than likely, the Germans would overrun their position.

Suddenly Hugh Redmond, moving quickly through the artillery fire, carrying wire on his back, dashed across a road leading to the River Waal. If he could stretch that wire out across the road, communications could be reestablished with headquarters and help might come for the embattled troops.

"He was real casual about it," said Dennis Eckles of Winslow, Arizona, another member of the communication platoon. "He had a smile on his face and he was acting as if he didn't have a care in the world, like this was the most routine thing to do."

"I remember him stretching the wire," said Pauli. "That was the last time I saw him."

The wire had been connected. Now Redmond reached the outer edge of the road on his way back to his comrades. A huge blast from a German 88-millimeter artillery piece shattered the earth around him, sending debris flying in all directions, knocking Redmond back and to his right. His right thigh, from just below the hip to just above the knee had been torn open and was bleeding profusely. He felt lightheaded. Noises around him were muffled. Now he heard movement around him, heard voices dimly. Medics were examining his deep wound, applying sulpha and making arrangements to move him back and away from the battle.

The 506th moved north again toward Arnhem. There the Germans counterattacked heavily. The British were unable to hold and Montgomery ordered the end of the expedition. MARKET-GARDEN would be considered a major defeat, a costly disaster for the Allies.

Later, the 506th gained glory in the drive to Germany, fighting bravely at Bastogne as their 101st leader, General McAuliffe, gained immortality by refusing a German offer to surrender when surrounded with a one word reply, "Nuts!" The 506th continued after Bastogne to Rheims, Mannheim, Starnberg and into Hitler's private playground at Berchtesgaden.

For Hugh Francis Redmond the war ended near the River Waal in Holland. He was removed to a hospital in Belgium. Amputation of his leg was considered. The doctors rejected that possibility and considered alternative treatments. He was flown to England for further therapy. There, on December 2, 1944, he was decorated with the Purple Heart with Bronze Oak Leaf Cluster for his two separate wounds in action against the enemy. In orders drafted at the Headquarters of the 188th U.S. General Hospital, Redmond was presented his medals. "By direction of the President, under provisions of AR 600-45, 22 September 1943, as amended, the Purple Heart with Bronze Oak Leaf Cluster is awarded to Corporal Hugh F. Redmond, 12142403, 506th Parachute Infantry, US Army for wounds received as a result of enemy action in Holland on 22 September 1944 and 6 October 1944."

Redmond remained under treatment in a hospital in England until early spring of 1945. He was shipped back to the United States for further treatment just before the war ended in May of 1945. Treatment continued at the base hospital in Camp Blanding, Florida. On May 7, 1945 Germany had signed a document of unconditional surrender at Rheims. On August 6, 1945 an atomic bomb was dropped on the Japanese city of Hiroshima. On August 9, 1945 a second atomic bomb was dropped on Nagasaki. Japan finally announced its surrender on August 14th and the official documents were signed on the Battleship Missouri in Tokyo Bay on September 2, 1945.

On October 18, 1945, still limping badly from his wound but able to walk, Redmond was separated from the service.

In twelve days he would be twenty six years old. Except for his leg wound, which doctors told him would eventually be completely healed, he was in good health. He had survived the war and matured as a man. He had left Yonkers as a factory worker without much direction in his life. He came back as a battle-scarred hero, a man of independence, proud of his accomplishments, secure in his own worth and certain of his priorities of home, family and country. There would be no way to measure the impact of his war experiences on his life, the death and destruction he had seen, the change in his ideas and ideals and the sense of self he had gained. He knew that he was as good as any man, better than most — able, intelligent and poised.

In reality, the impact of his war service, the 1124 days he had spent as a paratrooper, would be a significant factor in the character of Hugh Francis Redmond for the remainder of his life.

Chapter 10

Joining the CIA

Hugh Redmond was on his way home. The train rumbled north from Florida where he had been treated and discharged at Camp Blanding, moving along the East Coast and pulling into New York's Grand Central Station on October 19, 1945. Redmond, carrying his duffel bag over his right shoulder and his Army discharge papers in his left hand, pushed through the crowds of people meeting sons, brothers, fathers and husbands in the station. He walked slowly to the platform, dragging his injured right leg a little, looking for the local commuter train to Yonkers.

He emerged in the early evening twilight of that crisp October day at the Yonkers station, motioned for a cab and told the driver he was going to 65 Belmont Avenue. In ten minutes, he was in front of his house. He paid the one dollar cab fare and looked up at the house, noticing the old black fence had been painted white. Not much else had changed. He walked up the concrete steps slowly, put down his bag and rang the front door bell.

"He had never written us with his exact arrival time," says Ruth Boyle. "That was his way. He didn't want to put my mother and father out. He didn't want to have them come into New York or even to the Yonkers station to meet him."

His father seemed much older than he remembered him, looking more tired and worn than before. His mother, too, seemed more frail, her small glasses accentuating the boniness of her face. His sister Ruth was not there. She had married and was no longer living at home.

"He had small presents for all of us," Ruth remembers, "a scarf for mother, a wallet for our father, and handkerchiefs for me. He also got me in a corner when I came over that first night and said he had a very special gift for me."

"I brought this for you all the way from Holland," Hugh told his sister.

"What is it," she asked.

"Wait a second. Let me take it out of the box so you can see it."

"It looks like, well, I don't know, it looks like a piece of metal."

"That's what it is. A piece of metal. What makes it different is that it's the piece of metal that was in me. That's what the doctors took out of my leg in Holland. I want you to have it as a souvenir."

Redmond held the piece of shrapnel in his hand, rubbed it against his pants leg and gave it to his sister.

"That was sort of a joke," Ruth says. "Hugh thought I would be revolted by it. I wasn't. Actually, I was sort of amazed that things like that piece of shrapnel could be pulled out of people's bodies. I saved it in the box he gave me. I have it to this day."

The next day Redmond was back at Bebe's, back at Miller's store for cigarettes, back at the neighborhood bars, back with his friends. He picked up the routine of his life as he had left it, thinking occasionally about his future.

"I got home a little earlier than Hugh did," said Dick Falvey. "While I was away my parents started filling a jar with coins. When I got home we had a big blast with the money they had saved. The parties continued for a week with friends and relatives coming over to the house. I was just getting my feet on the ground about the time Hughie got home. I asked him what he planned to do now that the Army was through with him."

"I don't know, Muggsy. I gotta get a job with some action. I just can't sit around anymore," he said.

Redmond waited several weeks before he began looking for work. His leg still bothered him.

"He didn't complain," says Ruth Boyle, "but he limped badly. My father had arthritis and when it kicked up he would walk around the house with a cane. Once in a while Hugh would pick up that cane — especially if he had been standing at a bar with his friends all night — and use it to get around."

Jobs were difficult to find. Millions of young men were returning from service. The government stepped in and presented these young men with twenty dollars a week for fifty two weeks. The "fifty two — twenty club," as it was nicknamed, was an attempt to provide some money while these veterans adjusted to civilian life and found new jobs.

"I don't know what I'll do but I know what I won't do," Redmond told Dick Falvey one day. "I won't join the 52-20 club. I want to get a job soon — a real job, a job with action."

Falvey remembers that Redmond really was not much changed despite his wartime experiences, at least not on the outside. He looked the same, a bit heavier perhaps, with a few laugh lines on his face, but still strong, lean and chesty.

"About the only difference I saw," Falvey says, "was his attitude about working. He had been through a lot. He didn't want to work in a factory like he had before, or go into a quiet office job. He always said he wanted to go where the action was. That was the word he always used, 'action,' a job he could throw himself into, a job he could be proud to do."

One morning Redmond read a story in the paper about the building of the 9,117 foot long tunnel being constructed between Brooklyn and Manhattan Island — a massive project that had started before the war, stopped during the war and was now being resumed for completion before 1950. It mentioned that additional workers were being put on every day. The following morning Redmond borrowed his father's car and drove to Brooklyn. He went to the construction site of what would become known as the Brooklyn Battery Tunnel, and signed on as a laborer and assistant to the trained sandhogs.

Late in December he sat at a Yonkers bar with his friends, drinking beer, telling stories about the girls in France, watching the snow fall on Yonkers Avenue. One of his pals at the bar was Tommy Mulligan, an old friend from Roosevelt High School days. Mulligan asked Redmond how he was getting along at the construction job underground at the tunnel.

"It's a job, but I don't think I'm cut out to be a sandhog," Redmond told him.

"I know something you might be interested in," Tommy Mulligan said.

"What's that?"

"How about working for the government? They're looking for a lot of new young guys like us. They're expanding the OSS."

Mulligan had served in Europe during the war with the Office of Strategic Services. It was the first spy unit ever created by American Armed Forces. The agency had now come under civilian control and was run by the Department of State. OSS officers — in a year the name of the organization would be changed to the Central Intelligence Agency — were considered Foreign Service officers.

"I've got an application at home," Mulligan said. "Why don't you look it over?"

"Where do they serve?"

"All over. They're spreading out. Probably places like Germany, Japan, checking out the occupation troops, Africa, China, Australia, all over. C'mon over to the house tomorrow and take a look at the application."

On April 17, 1946, Hugh Francis Redmond journeyed to Washington, DC at government expense, went to the State Department, filled out an application for service as a courier in the OSS, passed a thorough physical examination and went through a briefing. He was told he would soon be hearing from the government.

"I remember the day he reported to Washington for his training," says Tommy Mulligan, the owner now of a bar outside New York's Green Haven Prison, called Tower 13. "It was April 30, 1946. The way I remember it is this: he was leaving that night on a train for Washington and that afternoon we went to Yankee Stadium for a baseball game between the Yankees and the Cleveland Indians. I was going to drive him to Grand Central after the game. I thought of going back in the OSS myself. I liked Europe. I had served in Germany. They didn't have any openings in Europe but they had a spot in China — Shanghai. I didn't want China. With Hugh it was different. He didn't care where he went. As long as he could have some action he would go anywhere they sent him."

The game at Yankee Stadium that afternoon, the last baseball game the two friends would ever share together, would not soon be forgotten.

"We were Yankee fans but Bobby Feller of Cleveland made that game memorable. He pitched a no-hitter against the Yankees and won the game 1-0 on a ninth inning home run by his catcher. I think it was the first time Feller had pitched in New York since returning from service. It was really an exciting day for Hugh and me. It sure planted that day firmly in our minds — yes, sir, April 30, 1946."

Redmond began intensive training for his job in the Office of Strategic Services. He was told his assignment would be to the American mission in China. He was briefed on the confusing conditions in China, the rise of the Communists in the country, the attempts by President Truman to reach a negotiated and reasonable settlement of the differences between the ruling Kuomintang of Chiang Kai-shek and the ambitious Communists under Mao Tse-tung. He was given training in the customs and conditions of the country. He was taught physical skills that he might find necessary. He underwent a vigorous physical training program destined to bring him back in strength and stamina to where he had been as a paratrooper before he was injured in Holland. He studied code books and learned to handle sophisticated communications machinery, more complicated than anything he had seen during military service. He worked and studied six long days a week, sometime sixteen to eighteen hours a day, absorbing the materials presented to him. He was given a crash course in Mandarin Chinese. He was mentally and physically tuned for his assignment.

On July 1 he was sent home for a month. He was to keep himself in top physical and mental condition, ready for his assignment at the end of that time, and was instructed to wait for a letter to be delivered to his home at the end of July which would include final instructions for his journey to China.

"He didn't talk about his new job," says Ruth Boyle. "He just told us he had a government position and would be going to China soon. He didn't know what he would do or how long he would be gone. My mother and father accepted it. After all, he was twenty six years old, single and knew what he wanted to do with his life."

Before he left Washington, Redmond filled out a form entitled, "Power of Attorney by individuals for collection of checks drawn on the Treasury of the United States." This form was to allow his mother to cash and use all his salary checks as she saw fit. They would be sent with his name to the Belmont Avenue address in Yonkers. His salary would be $7,500 a year to start. Any monies he needed in the operation of his duties in Washington, or later in Shanghai would be given to him in cash. The power of attorney would be granted officially on July 24, 1946. These monies were to be delivered to Mrs. Redmond continually during Hugh's lifetime. In addition, she would receive a check for $11.50 each month as a ten percent disability pension for Hugh's wartime injury.

Redmond came home and waited for his orders. He knew official word would not be coming from the government for a month. He talked with Bernie Connolly and Tommy Mulligan about his future job.

"You got some time before you have to go away," said Connolly. "Let's get a job in the mountains for a few weeks. I saw an ad in the paper this morning."

"Where's the place?"

"Tamiment. Up in the Poconos, a Jewish resort. We can get jobs there as busboys, make a few bucks and have a hell of a time. I hear there are a lot of lonely Jewish broads up there."

The following morning Hugh Redmond, Bernie Connolly and Tommy Mulligan drove downtown to Manhattan to apply for jobs as busboys at Tamiment. Redmond was the spokesman as they entered the camp office. A small middle aged woman sat behind a desk piled high with papers. She had gray hair and wore thick glasses.

"Hi, Honey," Redmond said. "We're here to apply for those jobs as busboys."

"Do you have your applications filled out?"

"Sure do. Here they are."

"Now, are you all college students, as required for this job?"

"Right. I'm studying law at NYU. My friend here is studying medicine at Fordham and my other friend here is studying mathematics at Columbia."

"You know you have to stay until Labor Day. When does your college semester resume?"

"Isn't that funny? None of us has to be in school until the week after Labor Day."

"We need help right away. You all look like strong boys and I'm going to give you the jobs. Be here tomorrow morning at 8:30 with your things and we'll drive you to work."

"Great. That's real nice of you, honey," said Redmond. "We certainly do appreciate your confidence and we know we'll have a good time in the mountains."

Mulligan, Connolly and Redmond walked out of the small office into the summer heat of New York.

"Charmed her, didn't I?" said Redmond.

"I think you're in love," said Connolly.

"The secret of getting a job is making the person hiring you think *they* are in love with *you*," said Redmond.

The three young men were driven up to the resort in the Pocono Mountains of eastern Pennsylvania the next morning. By noon they had been assigned to quarters that were similar to the Army barracks they all knew so well. They were to work as busboys, help the waiters set up tables, clear dishes, bring extra food from the kitchen and clean and clear tables. In exchange they were paid two dollars a day, earned tips and were given free room and board. They averaged fifty dollars a week. They were also allowed use of the private lake and boats, asked to dance with guests in the socials at night and given enough time off to enjoy the fresh air and sunshine.

"It was an adult camp," says Connolly. "They had a lot of those rich Jewish girls up there looking for husbands. Some of them got tired of the same Jewish guys they knew in the city and were happy to go off with us as a novelty. They knew we weren't about to marry them but we had nothing against a good time in the woods with them. We had all been through the war, had all kinds of experiences with women. We could handle ourselves with anybody. Hugh was the best. He would come on sort of quiet and shy, then start charming them with his wit and have them right where he wanted them in no time at all. He was really having a hell of a summer. One of the women up there, a daughter or wife of the owner, I forget which fell in love with him. I mean he was really having a great time with her, and she was just loving the whole thing. There was nothing she wouldn't do for old Hughie and his pals after that.

The days passed quickly. The month of July was hot but beautiful. Redmond worked faithfully at his summer job and thoroughly enjoyed his free time. Soon he would receive the letter that was going to change his life, and he looked forward to it.

"He kept talking about the new job, about going where the action is, about doing something important," says Bernie Connolly. "I remember one night we were laying around the bunk and he seemed distracted. Finally he looked up at me and he said, 'Bernie, this is an important job I'm taking. It really matters to me. I think I can help this country.' He felt that. Felt it very deeply. He cared, he really cared about doing something for his country. Maybe it was his way of giving back to the country that had done so much for him."

On the second day of August, 1946, the special delivery letter he had been eagerly looking forward to arrived at the camp, forwarded from his home in Yonkers. He opened it in front of Connolly and Mulligan. "This is it," he said excitedly, "my orders to China."

Connolly, Mulligan and Redmond left Tamiment together. They had made an agreement with each other to stay only until Hugh received his orders.

"There was no point in staying any longer," says Connolly. "We had come up to have a good time for a month. If we weren't going to be together we would go home. It was about time we all got serious jobs anyway."

Redmond had a couple of days to get his things together, to say good-bye to friends and family, to end one part of his life and to start a new one.

"I remember him coming over that night," says Dick Falvey. "He was really thrilled. He could not have been more excited. The job just seemed wonderful to him. It was important, he would have adventure and he would be doing something worthwhile. It gave him great pride."

Falvey said they shared a few beers that last night, laughed over old times, and wished each other well in the years to come.

"How could I know that night that I would never see Hugh Redmond again?" asked Falvey. "He was so happy, so excited about the whole thing, so full of youth and life. He even wanted me to join up. I had a job with the railroad and I had had my fill of world travel during the war, but he was persuasive. I thought about going but then the beer wore off. I wish there were ways of knowing things like that at the time. I wish I could have said something dramatic to him — to tell him what a good pal he had been, to tell him how much I thought about him in all those years afterwards."

Falvey said he heard from Redmond only once after he left Yonkers for his life in the Far East.

"He sent me a postcard. It was one of those things you have made up in tourist places. He was standing in front of the Taj -Mahal in India. He had a big grin on his face. He seemed about the happiest man in the world. The card just said, 'It's all very exciting. Wish you were here."

Redmond was doing some final shopping chores before his trip and was taking the trolley back from downtown Yonkers when he ran into Vince Sackett. Sackett was on summer vacation from his studies at Maryknoll. He hoped to be ordained and sent to China as a missionary. All of Redmond's close friends knew he was headed for China to work for the government.

"I caught his eye just as he was getting off the trolley," remembers Sackett. "We knew he was leaving in a day or so. I wanted to wish him well, I wanted to say something for the occasion. 'See you in Shanghai,' I said. A lot of people on the trolley heard me say it. They looked up. They seemed surprised. Kids from Yonkers just don't meet casually in Shanghai. They just don't."

Hugh's mother and father, Ruth and her new husband all gathered for a final dinner with Hugh the night before his trip. Hugh's favorite, a shrimp dinner was served and much beer was drunk in celebration of Hugh's new career. The old man sang some fine old Irish songs and everybody was in wonderful humor. Hughie laughed a lot and told some funny stories about his experiences in Europe. He was high from too much beer and wine.

"Mother," he suddenly said, in a serious tone, "I'll make you proud of me." Then they all got ready to leave. Redmond had to get up early the next morning to catch a train for San Francisco where he would board a ship for China.

On August 12, 1946, shortly before noon on a pleasant summer afternoon in San Francisco, Hugh Francis Redmond walked up the gang-plank of the United States ocean liner *President Abraham Lincoln*. He carried an American passport and business cards identifying him as a buyer for Henningsen Produce Company of New York and Shanghai, China.

Chapter *11*

Secrets of Shanghai

Shanghai was a city of international intrigue, of adventure, of sin, of severe foreign exploitation of the local Chinese by governments, businesses and individuals. Masses of humanity filled the wide avenues and side streets along Nanking Road. In the middle of the 1920s Shanghai was teeming with more than three million people. The power struggle among the Western nations for control of the city was legendary. The city always had a reputation for being overrun by international spies, kidnapers, (hence the term to be Shanghaied), murderers, profiteers, hustlers, con men of every political stripe. Shanghai had grown to be the meeting ground for almost every international form of evil. It was a port city on the South China Sea with its main commerce and industry developing on the left bank of the Hwang Pu River. Much of the city was surrounded by a river front drive known as the Bund. In the 1920s it was choking with people, rickshaws, wagons, some American made automobiles, animals and garbage. It was, in effect, two cities in one: the well-cared for, culturally separated International Quarter run by the British, French, Germans and Americans, with some smaller colonies of White Russians, Portuguese, Scandinavians and Eastern Europeans and the densely populated Chinese Quarter — filled with the impoverished, who lived with constant hunger and squalor.

With its proximity to the sea and the world beyond and its access to the mass markets of China through the Yangtze River, Shanghai had never achieved political unity or peace. Foreign governments and local war lords ripped it apart for generations. The uneducated masses of

Chinese were apolitical, showing quick loyalty to whatever war lord, whatever foreign devil, would give them enough yuan for a bowl of rice and a cup of tea.

"Shanghai was an exciting city, a wonderful city when I first went there in 1925," said Kent Lutey, a tall, dignified, mustachioed man who had been an executive with the Henningsen Produce Company of Shanghai for nearly a dozen years. "The Chinese are great people, hard working people. The only problem is, there are just too many of them."

The overcrowding, the exploitation by the war lords and the foreigners, the sickness, the disease, the discomforts, would naturally lead to incredible unrest. The uneducated Chinese could not really know what avenues of remedy to seek. They only knew that life was brutally hard for them.

After the Russian Revolution in 1917, many Chinese traveled to Moscow to learn the new ways of their Communist masters. Among these visitors to Russia was a tall, handsome young man by the name of Chiang Kai-shek. He dreamed of making China an idealistic state. Through disillusionment with the Russians, disagreements with his own comrades and overt ambition and hunger for power, Chiang had broken with the Communists. As he gained and solidified his power, he reinforced the ruling political party, the Kuomintang, in his own image, hunted down Communists and destroyed them as enemies of the state. As he gained greater strength politically, and as unrest grew in Shanghai, a solid core of Chinese Communists attempted to gain control of the city. Chiang put an end to that in 1927 when he sent more than a hundred thousand of his troops racing through Shanghai on a mission of death. The soldiers were to ferret out Communists and kill them on sight. More than six thousand people were murdered in Shanghai by Chiang's orders, many of them in their own homes before wives and children, still others on the streets, in full view of astonished and horrified crowds. Slaughter took place, often with no evidence of any Communist party affiliation, done simply at the whim of the Nationalist cadre.

The American community, protected by the high walls of the International Quarter, demanded help from the home government.

Marines and cavalry units, under the command of General Smedley Butler, were landed by sea and proceeded to protect the homes and businesses of the international community. They wore World War I spats and uniforms, carried Springfield rifles with glistening sabers at their sides, giving rise to some of the more romantic adventure stories of the 1920s. They were the cream of the small group of American professional soldiers.

Chiang denounced the presence of American troops on Chinese soil but his weak, faction-ridden army could do little to move them out. Then, in 1932, flushed with militarism and ambition, Japan bombed Shanghai under the pretext of protecting Japanese interests in the city. Chiang immediately turned to the American forces for protection against the Japanese. The Japanese took control of the city completely in 1937. China and Japan were at war. Shanghai would remain under Japanese rule until 1945.

On a pleasant winter afternoon in New York, Kent Lutey dined at the Princeton Club and recalled those days of extra-territoriality in Shanghai, the days of international intrigue, those days of American exploitation and colonialism of the Chinese.

"Henningsen Produce Company was a small operation when I got there in '25. I was born in Phillipsburg, Montana and went to school in the East at the Wharton School of the University of Pennsylvania. The business, a small China trade company then, was involved in getting fresh eggs, drying them and shipping them to the rest of China, Japan and Europe. My father had been a good friend of A.P. Henningsen, who had started the company with his brother Victor, in 1920. When I got out of school I was offered a job with them and took a steamship out of San Francisco to join the group," Lutey said.

Lutey moved into a house on Dinwell Road just outside the International Quarter, in an area called Hongpew, which was populated mostly by French businessmen.

"It was easy to tell when you were out of the International Quarter and in the Chinese section," Lutey said. "As soon as the paved road ended and the dirt roads began, that was the Chinese Quarter."

Lutey worked in the egg division of the company for several years. He would get home leave every three years, for three months. One month of it was vacation and the other two months were spent back in the company's home office in Portland, Oregon.

"While I was out in Oregon one year, the general manager of the company, Ulysses S. Harksen, asked me if I thought we could develop another division."

Lutey was assigned the task of developing the ice cream division, hiring the help, managing the equipment, developing a plan for distribution throughout China.

"Our biggest problem," he said "was an educational one. The Chinese would not eat anything that wasn't cooked. They cooked absolutely everything. They would accept a frozen product if they knew that it needed to be cooked before they ate it. We got around the problem with a long educational program showing them how frozen products stayed fresh and were healthy."

The ice cream factory was established on Sawgin Road some three hundred yards from the gates of the International Quarter. It was a three story wooden building with two stories for factory and equipment and one story for office use. The largest building in Shanghai at the time was the six story Hong Kong-Shanghai bank, built by the British. There were three or four Americans running the factory and more than two thousand Chinese employed as laborers. They were paid one dollar a day in silver coin since the workers didn't trust the constant fluctuation of the Chinese equivalent of the dollar, the yuan.

"We got along very well with our Chinese employees," Lutey said. "They were happy to have the jobs. There were no anti-American sentiments at that time. Chiang tried to create some in '27 when he came up from Canton but the way he massacred the Communists turned even his own people away from him. Then when the Japanese bombed Shanghai in '32 he became very friendly. In '37 when the Japanese invaded the city, they burned our factory to the ground."

Lutey remembers life in Shanghai from 1925 through 1937 as very pleasant and comfortable for American businessmen.

"There were some marvelous hotels — the Cathay, the Metropole, the Astor House and the Palace. There were dances every weekend. We all lived in these very comfortable homes, complete with house boys and maids. The American colony was pretty good size. Standard Oil, American Tobacco, Chase Bank and many other large companies had people stationed there. Life was most enjoyable. They had a chit system that I had never seen before or since. You could buy anything with a chit — taxi cab rides, meals in restaurants, drinks in night clubs, cigarettes, even call girls. The chit system finally disappeared when too many Chinese taxi drivers started showing up at too many American offices to redeem their chits from American employees."

Lutey remembers Shanghai as a very sophisticated city with many cultural activities within the International Quarter.

"Every Saturday night there was a black tie dance at the Cathay Hotel. Every Sunday there was a polo game or a fox hunt. There were concerts and plays to see. I never was so well dressed as when I lived in China. My clothes all came from Hong Kong and the tailor would come to my house for three or four fittings. Everything was beautifully detailed and fit superbly."

Lutey left Shanghai in 1945. He was freed by the Chinese after being held prisoner by the Japanese during World War II. He never returned to China, and he has had no contact with the Henningsen Produce Company since his return to America after the war.

"Had you ever heard the name Hugh Francis Redmond at any time after your return to America?" he was asked.

"Only in news reports after I left the country. He was identified as an employee of Henningsen and that caught my eye," said Lutey.

"If he did work for Henningsen, if he was a legitimate American businessman as the government said in 1946 in Shanghai, what might he have done?"

"Let me see. He was twenty six or twenty seven years old at the time, you say, about the same age I was when I first went to China. He might have been a junior executive, a trainee in the ice cream division. Yes, he could well have been an ice cream man. In Chinese he would be known as 'the bing-a-ling man.'"

Only one man, the late U.S. Harksen, general manager of the Henningsen Produce Company in 1946, knew that Hugh Francis Redmond worked for the government and was using the Henningsen Produce Company as a pre-arranged cover for his spy activities in Shanghai.

"I got to China in 1931," said Laurist V. Larsen, former operations chief of the company, now retired and living in Palo Alto, California. "I left just before the Communists took over China in 1949. I had seen Redmond several times. I didn't know what he did. I assumed he was one of our trainees. It was a common thing to have American spies over there at the time, using all kinds of companies as cover. I remember Harksen mentioning Redmond's name to me once. I can't remember in what connection. Things started getting pretty confusing there in 1949. I remember just before the Communists took over that Harksen told me he had recommended to Redmond that he leave the country. Then Harksen said Redmond told him, 'I've got good contacts. I can get out any time I want.' Harksen let it go at that."

Redmond had made most of his contacts with Nationalist sympathizers in the early days of 1947. China was in revolution. The American mediation effort had crumbled, General Marshall's attempt at bringing the Communists and the Nationalists together had failed and the country was in turmoil.

Redmond lived quietly in a small apartment in the Chinese section of the city overlooking the Bund. Slowly, carefully, as an experienced communications expert, he acquired radio equipment and had hidden receiving and sending apparatus in his apartment. He was in constant contact with the American mission in Shanghai and with his superiors in Hong Kong. He reported on the deteriorating condition of Nationalist forces in Shanghai. He increased his daily contacts with Nationalist undercover forces. In regular clandestine meetings with Nationalist sources, he learned of their own movements and of the Communist advances. He helped evacuate Nationalist politicians and leaders as the Communists began surfacing in the city. On occasion he would travel north to Peiping, under the guise of business for Henningsen, explore the situation there, communicate with other Nationalist forces and make low level contacts with other members of the American services. A huge spy network, consisting of others like himself posing as businessmen, sympathetic missionaries and church officials, students, journalists and travelers, were being formed throughout the country as Communist strength grew.

In the early 1920s, Chiang had as an ally a husky, intellectual farmer's son named Mao Tse-tung, who had visited Russia and envisioned a Communist state in China led by and set up for peasants, that untapped mass of Chinese strength. After the alliance between Chiang and Mao disintegrated, Mao was hunted throughout China. He escaped death many times. His small band of followers were trapped in the province of Juichin in southern China in 1934. The Nationalists attempted to starve the Communists out after they were encircled and put an end once and for all to the only viable alternative to Chiang's regime. Deciding neither to fight nor wait for starvation to destroy his forces, Mao, in a brilliant move, marched some forty thousand men under the cover of darkness out of their southern hideouts and journeyed north. They crossed some six thousand miles of China and eleven provinces, over impossibly difficult terrain, with his forces swelling to more than a hundred thousand along the way. Mao's forces were pursued by Chiang's men. These troops sick, hungry and worn, the tattered survivors of this ragtag army, perhaps some forty five thousand strong, arrived in the northern province in the summer of 1935. The Communist revolution had survived in the person of these men and was to wend its way back through all of China for final victory in 1949.

Mao's men had closed to within several miles of Shanghai in the early spring of 1949.

"You could hear the shelling of the large Communist guns from the north bank of the Yangtze River," said Ralph Olmstead, general manager of the Henningsen Produce Company from 1945 to 1949.

Olmstead, with varied government and business experience, had worked as an advisor to Chiang under the auspices of General Marshall.

He was closely identified with the American decision to back Chiang against Mao after relations between the two Chinese leaders erupted in open revolution. American public opinion was now strongly against Mao and the Communists. Olmstead knew he would be in serious difficulty if he did not leave China immediately.

"The Chinese had as good an intelligence system as ours — maybe better," he said. "They knew where the foreigners were. China has always been a difficult country for a Westerner to hide in. I had to leave. I was too well known as a supporter of Chiang. My name had been on the radio too often and my picture had been in the paper."

Olmstead, living in retirement near a golf course in North Carolina, said he left Shanghai by rail just three days before the Communists occupied the city.

"We tried to keep the company going when I left," he said. "We left the office manager, a man named A.M. Gonsalves, in charge of operations. Gonsalves had a Portuguese passport and we hoped the Communists would allow the company to continue under his control."

The Communists made no overt moves against the company after they took over Shanghai in May of 1949. Through manipulation of the Chinese labor force, through extra taxes, frustrating red tape and constant surveillance, they increased the pressures on the Henningsen company. Gonsalves continued to run the Henningsen operation until 1950. He was finally arrested, held for a short while and allowed to leave. He now lives in South America.

Communist forces moved into Shanghai in great numbers late in May. The last major stronghold of the Nationalists, the city of Canton, fell in September. Mao declared a Communist state and complete victory in his quarter century struggle against Chiang in October as the Nationalists retreated to Formosa.

Under orders from his superiors in the Central Intelligence Agency, Hugh Redmond continued on in Shanghai under Communist rule. His cover as an employee of Henningsen was tenuous at best now, with the company business almost totally concerned with collection of old accounts and closing down of the entire operation. The American government chose not to recognize the new Communist state and the American mission in Shanghai was confiscated by the Communists. Redmond's main duties were to keep his American contacts in Hong Kong informed of the dramatic changes in the city. Only through its network of spies could the United States get any line on the activities, movements and ambitions of the new enemy nation. Redmond increased his contacts, now under most dangerous conditions for himself and his sources, Nationalists who chose to remain in China. The American government still clung to the fantasy of Chiang's return to the mainland. Redmond was a significant instrument in their China policy.

Always a city of many conflicting sides and appearances, Shanghai, in 1949, was one of the most confusing places on earth.

John Leighton Stuart, the last American ambassador to China, described some of the conditions in his book, *Fifty Years in China.*

> *"Nanking having fallen quickly to the Communists,"* Stuart wrote, *"they were virtually compelled to follow on at once to Shanghai. They were well aware of course of the international economic, administrative and other problems focusing in that swollen Eurasian metropolis...The physical efforts (of the Nationalists) were wastefully executed. But the treatment of Shanghai residents and its psychological consequences were even worse. Secret service agents hunted down persons suspected of leftist leanings. Prominent citizens thought of as ready to negotiate with the Communists for a peaceful turnover were forced to withdraw to Hong Kong or fled there for safety. Special 'contributions' for defense measures were extracted from all according to ability to pay, and this became a form of private extortion as well. Vessels and vehicles were commandeered. Houses were razed, trees cut down, thoroughfares barricaded, posters and parades enforced in order to win popular support. Silver dollars were paid and movie tickets and other special privileges were given or promised to soldiers for the*

same purpose. Communist agents were meanwhile active underground. The Generalissimo's hold upon his followers was, however, strong enough to galvanize the defense forces into some measure of co-ordination and to inspire in them more of the will to fight than had been shown in previous battles where it would have been worthwhile. Within a few weeks, however, the Communists were able to claim Shanghai.

The Ambassador continues,

"I wanted to see Shanghai under the new control and specially to confer with American nationals...The impression of Shanghai during these first days of Communist rule was that they had taken control with vigor, competence and incorruptibility, but their propaganda against American imperialism and on behalf of the less privileged masses would provoke labor disturbances that might become serious, and that their combination of both Nationalistic and Marxist fanaticism, clashing against the economic structure of this cosmopolitan city and the practical exigencies of keeping five million people fed and protected, would make of Shanghai a very significant experimental laboratory.

Stuart goes on to describe the incredible conditions under which British and American business-men attempted to continue normal commerce under the Communist rule.

"The incidents involving British, American and other foreigners in Shanghai became increasingly troublesome. These were usually provoked by the general labor unrest. The sudden insistence on the use of the Chinese language only in what began as a foreign settlement where English had been almost indispensable was disconcerting to what remained of the foreign population. The victims were subject to rough manhandling and abusive tirades which were insulting and humiliating in the

extreme. They were forced to sign statements and make apologies which were gloatingly published in the local press together with obscene distortions of the facts. All this may be regarded as a bit of sociological case study. The British chiefly had affected an attitude of contemptuous racial superiority, quite in the Kipling tradition toward Chinese people and their civilization. There was increasing Communist anti-foreign, notably anti-American propaganda, describing us all as grasping imperialists. The foreigners who had stayed on in Shanghai rather than respond to arrangements for evacuation had done so in the main because of their friendly feelings for the Chinese.

Stuart continues

"...The trends in Communist policy led me to recommend to the State Department that plans be made to evacuate Americans from Communist-controlled areas, especially Shanghai. Missionaries who had not already left China were in general ready to face the unknown in the spirit which had originally led them to this career and with the hope that the very fact of staying on under unpromising conditions might in itself be an effective form of witness bearing.

"But for the businessmen,"

Stuart wrote,

"the outlook was bleak indeed, unrelieved by any idealistic aims."

Hugh Francis Redmond, posing as an American businessman, a 'bing-a-ling man,' was constantly under surveillance.

The American colony grew smaller and smaller through the early days of 1950. Businessmen left on every ship that came and went from Shanghai. Missionaries, with some few exceptions, were called home. Redmond almost always stayed indoors. His meetings with Chinese businessmen were all clandestine. His transmissions to his superiors, through hidden radio networks, were made mostly in the early hours before daybreak when the city was still and the chance of detection was at a minimum. Through quick contacts with other agents passing through the city, he was supplied with money and papers to help anti-Communist Chinese slip out of Shanghai, some by train to Canton and on to Hong Kong, some by ship, a few by small planes and a few even by tiny boats. The pressures increased as the Communists became more openly hostile with foreigners.

Redmond never allowed any of these problems to get through his tough exterior when communicating with his family back home. In early June of 1950, he wrote, "life goes on here pleasantly as always. The fighting that we had last year has ceased. The pace of the city seems to be slowing down with the coming of summer heat. Business is good and I am well."

On June 25, 1950, troops from North Korea poured across the 38th parallel to be met, under orders of Harry S. Truman and by command of the United Nations in New York, by a combined army of American and South Korean soldiers. In some four months, more than one hundred thousand pajama-clad Chinese troops would charge across the Yalu River in North Korea to drive back the advancing United Nations forces.

On that summer day in June, the fate of Hugh Francis Redmond would be fixed.

Chapter 12

Prisoner of the Reds

The Communists tightened their stranglehold on the city of Shanghai in the early days of 1951. Communication to the outside world became more difficult. The intensity of the propaganda, especially anti-American propaganda as a direct result of the Korean war, increased severely. Posters filled the walls of buildings showing American soldiers slicing the heads off Chinese babies. Passion was at a fever pitch. Fear gripped millions of residents, mostly non-political, uneducated, unsophisticated Chinese who knew little or nothing of the revolution sweeping their country. All former Nationalist Chinese party members had been forced to register with the Communist police officials.

A Chinese businessman named Robert Loh, who was later to slip out of China and write of those days in his book, *Escape From China*, pointed out the cruel methods of the Communists

> *"...all the ex-Nationalists had registered. Without warning then, the authorities arrested them all. Most of those arrested were executed or punished secretly. Few were held for trial. Those brought to trial were always actual gangsters or corrupt politicians. The trials followed the same pattern as the meetings on land reform. The cadres assembled a crowd by ordering the residents of an area to appear in a specified public place. Planned activists led the people in shouting abusive slogans. Handcuffed prisoners were brought out and made to kneel before the masses. Communist officials opened the trial with a speech denouncing the accused and listing his crimes.*

*Previously arranged accusers then came forward to tell,
vividly and often sincerely, their grievances. The crowd,
harangued by the activists, were worked up to a frenzied
screaming, 'KILL THE COUNTER REVOLUTIONAR-
IES, KILL, KILL, KILL.' Thereupon the officials in
response to the will of the masses ordered the prisoners
to be killed. Usually the sentence was carried out at once
in front of the crowd."*

On April 21, Redmond, working closely with Nationalist friends, arranged for more than seven thousand dollars to be passed to businessmen for use in arranging for their covert transportation from Shanghai to Taipei on a cargo ship registered out of Cuba.

On April 22, 1951, Redmond received a coded message from his superiors in Hong Kong. The message, communicated by voice and received in his apartment at 2:33 A.M. simply said, "ENJOY THE DANCE."

This was a pre-arranged signal. Redmond had been ordered out of Shanghai by the Central Intelligence Agency. It was no longer considered safe for Redmond to operate in the midst of a Chinese Communist city. Conditions had worsened and the loss by death or imprisonment of an agent of Redmond's dedication, skills and loyalties would be a severe blow to the Agency and to its operations in China and the Far East.

In order not to arouse suspicion or alert the Communists to any of his prior activities, Redmond was ordered to leave through normal channels. He was booked as a passenger on the American ship, the *General Gordon,* which had been making two runs a month out of Shanghai with American passengers. The Chinese closely scrutinized passengers leaving the city. They confiscated most property of worth, but were not unhappy about the American evacuation. The city of Shanghai would be even more firmly in Communist hands once all foreigners, especially Americans, were removed from the city.

On April 26, 1951, carrying one small suitcase and papers identifying him as an American citizen and an employee of Henningsen Produce Company in their ice cream division, Redmond hailed a cab and was taken to the waterfront. The *General Gordon* was some 30 minutes from sailing. There seemed no special unrest, no extra concentration of guards at the docks. Redmond felt that things were going smoothly. After more than four and a half years in China, Redmond was on his way home.

He had made only one mistake.

Thirty seven days earlier he had married an attractive, dark-haired, brown eyed piano teacher who lived in Shanghai since her family's escape from White Russia. Her name was Lena Petrov and she was with him as he paid the driver, pulled out his small suitcase and walked to the gangplank.

"Your papers, please," said a burly Chinese official in civilian clothes.

Redmond reached for his American passport, although the Chinese no longer considered it a valid travel document, except under their own terms.

The official studied his papers, looking at Redmond's photograph and his face. He said nothing. He motioned for Lena's papers. He examined them closely. He motioned for her to move up the gangplank. Redmond moved to follow.

"Over here, Mr. Redmond, please."

"I must stay with my wife," Redmond said. "Her English is not that good."

"Follow me, please. Your wife will be cared for."

Redmond swallowed hard. Keeping his face immobile, he looked up at Lena. He could see tears forming in her eyes. He felt the sharp, cold thrust of a handgun in his right side. He licked his lips, turned back toward the ship for an instant, then followed the Chinese official.

He was taken to a small police office at the end of the dock and told to stand facing a wall. Then he was searched. His bag was taken from him. The officials who had arrested him disappeared. He could hear the sounds of deck hands assisting the *General Gordon* as it left its berth and sailed into the China Sea. It was a little after noon on April 26, 1951.

Three days later the phone rang in the early hours of the evening at the Redmond home in Yonkers. Mrs. Redmond was tired from a full day of work as the cafeteria manager in a Yonkers school. She had been rolling cabbage leaves and dried her hands as she walked slowly to the phone.

"Hello," she said.

"Mother, this is Hughie."

"Hughie, how are you?"

"I'm calling from Shanghai. I hope to be on my way home soon."

"That's wonderful. When can we expect you."

"I don't know for sure yet. I'm having some trouble with my papers. I have some news for you. I've married. My wife will be in Yonkers soon. She is on her way home."

"Your *wife*? When did you get married? What is her name?"

Ruth Boyle's description of the telephone call her mother received that early evening from her brother indicated there was nothing to be concerned about.

"My mother said he sounded quite normal on the phone. The news about his marriage was a shock, since that was the first we'd heard of it. We knew he would marry sooner or later. After all, Hugh was thirty one now. We hadn't seen him for nearly five years and he was never one to talk about his girl friends," she said.

Lena Petrov Redmond arrived in Yonkers and moved in with the Redmonds. The relationship was untenable from the start. There was no further word from Hugh — no more calls, no letters, no communication in any form.

Once the young Mrs. Redmond arrived in Yonkers, she made herself at home in the senior Redmond's house. They noticed that Lena seemed unconcerned about her husband. She read American magazines, took long walks, and did little to help around the house. She spent her time watching television. She talked about how much she missed having a piano. Finally she got a job in Yonkers as a private piano teacher with lessons in the homes of her pupils.

"She was uncommunicative," recalls Ruth Boyle. "Without Hugh there to make a connection, there was no real relationship between Lena and us, and there was little to talk about. She was used to a different life in Shanghai. She had servants there, ready to cater to her every need. Once she came here, she treated mother as though she were just another servant."

The days went by slowly. There was no word from Hugh. The petty bickering between Lena and Mrs. Redmond grew worse. Finally, tired of being treated like a servant in her own home, Mrs. Redmond asked Lena to leave the house and to find her own apartment. The Redmonds wanted to return to their private lives.

Lena Petrov Redmond moved out. She got an apartment in Yonkers and she continued to teach the piano. Later, she moved to Milwaukee and then on to Hampton, Virginia. One day papers arrived at the Redmond home in Yonkers. The Redmonds learned that Lena Petrov had divorced Hugh Redmond, charging abandonment. She had slipped completely out of their lives.

It would be years later before the Redmond family became aware of the most crushing blow of all. A CIA agent told a friend of Redmond's that Lena had been a double agent. She was working for the Communists as well as for us. No one knew it at the time, but Lena Petrov Redmond had betrayed Hugh Redmond.

The days passed slowly for the Redmonds. There was no word from Hugh and no indication from the government that they knew he had been detained, or that they cared. The Redmonds sat back quietly and waited. They didn't know where to turn. They knew Hugh worked for the government but they didn't quite know what he did. They knew he was in Shanghai. They knew, from his phone call, that he hadn't been allowed to leave.

"That was the worst part," said Ruth Boyle. "Just not knowing."

As the intensity of fighting in the Korean War increased, reporters made constant inquiries of the United States State Department about civilian and military prisoners of the Koreans and the Chinese. On May 21, 1951, less than a month after Hugh Redmond had been seized by the Chinese Communists in Shanghai, the Department of State in bulletin number 414 delivered to the press a statement concerning "AMERI-CANS DETAINED BY COMMUNIST AUTHORITIES IN CHINA."

"The Department of State has been extremely concerned for an extended period of time," the statement read, "over the imprisonment by Chinese Communist authorities of a number of American nationals, now believed to number more than thirty. At least some of these are definitely known to have been allowed no communication with anyone outside. In most cases the local Chinese Communist authorities have given no explanation of the arrests or any information concerning the welfare or whereabouts of the persons arrested. The Department of State has also been concerned for some time over the continued denial by Chinese Communist authorities of exit permits to some Americans, including a number of Shanghai businessmen, some of whom have been endeavoring for a year to leave China. Arbitrary refusal to permit aliens to depart from a country is, of course, a violation of the elementary principles of international law and practice."

Redmond was being held in a house at 13 Kao Yu Road in Shanghai with two French priests, two other Americans and one British businessman. Each day he was fed one small bowl of rice, one bowl of salted vegetables, a hard piece of bread and one small cup of bitter tea. He slept on a cold bare wooden floor. Conditions were not sanitary. He was beaten about his lower back and kidneys with wooden sticks. The windows were sealed tight in the house and there was no fresh air. He was questioned constantly by teams of interrogators. He was forced to read propaganda statements aloud. He was questioned about his associates in China and his spying activities. He said nothing. He insisted he was a legitimate American businessman working for Henningsen Produce Company and demanded they free him and allow him to return to the United States where he could rejoin his wife.

"All they wanted him to do was sign this piece of paper saying he had been a spy, and they probably would have let him go," said Father John McCormack, an elderly missionary from Maryknoll who was under house arrest with Redmond in Shanghai. "He was the bravest man I have ever known. It brought tears to my eyes to see what they were doing to this fine young man."

A United States Senator, William F. Knowland of California, was moved by the issue of the American prisoners. He began to make inquiries at the State Department. Under the conditions existing at the time, Knowland, an ally of the infamous Senator Joseph McCarthy of Wisconsin, had a great deal of power. He doggedly pursued the issue. He demanded information on the prisoners, urging the State Department to work harder with their British contacts in an attempt to obtain the names of Americans held by the Communists. It was an issue that had great public support and popular appeal.

In early October of 1951 Knowland received a promising note from an assistant secretary of the State Department by the name of Dean Rusk. Rusk had told Knowland that the State Department might soon be able to come up with some names. Knowland wrote Rusk asking that the matter be pressed harder with the British, who represented us with the Communist government of China. On October 19th, Rusk sent a confidential memo to Knowland listing the names of Americans held by the Communists. He asked Knowland to keep this list a secret. On November 30, 1951, Knowland sent a wire to Rusk asking for permission to release the names. On December 1st, Rusk wrote Knowland that whatever information was available about these prisoners at the State Department would be forwarded to the Senator from California. On December 7, 1951, Knowland chose to release the names of some thirty Americans — mostly missionaries, long time residents of China and people of mixed parentage with some Chinese blood. The only name on the list who was neither a missionary, a life long businessman in China nor had any Chinese heritage, was Hugh Francis Redmond.

"That was the first word we had that Hugh was actually a prisoner and the first word that the government knew of his situation," said Ruth Boyle. "We were very grateful to Senator Knowland."

The State Department, deeply concerned that investigation of Redmond's background would reveal no previous business experience before China, and possibly lead to his CIA connection, reacted sharply to Knowland's release of the names.

Under Secretary of State James E. Webb wrote a scathing letter to Senator Knowland. "It is with deep regret," the letter began, "that I learned of your release to the press of the names of the American citizens imprisoned in Communist China. Mr. Rusk sent you this list in confidence. He explained to you that it was the considered judgment of the Department that the list should not be made public. As a United States Senator, you have in the past been given access to classified information on the understanding that it was not to be released to the public. Although the question of whether particular information should or should not be made public may be susceptible to an honest difference of opinion, the decision must be made by the person responsible. I regret that in this instance you chose to disregard this fundamental principle and to take independent action."

With the release of Redmond's name, conditions grew worse for him. He was still being held under house arrest at 13 Kao Yu Road but he was now completely segregated from other prisoners.

"Several of us had been kept together in one large room," said Father McCormack. "Now Mr. Redmond was moved into a separate, small room. Hardly a day went by when we couldn't hear screams of pain. Weeks would go by when we wouldn't see him. Then he would be allowed to walk in the courtyard for a few minutes, usually away from the rest of us. He was always bound. He would nod, offer a weak smile and say nothing."

The Communists were certain Redmond was an American spy. What they did not know was with whom he had communicated. Lena Petrov could give them times and dates of Redmond's communications. She could never give them names. They worked hard to break Redmond. They withheld food. They abused him physically. They kept at him with teams of interrogators for days on end. They deprived him of sleep. He grew weaker. He would only say, "I am an American businessman. I am employed by the Henningsen Produce Company. I do not know why I am being held."

More than eighteen months after Redmond had been arrested, a second team of United States CIA agents was captured by the Chinese. CIA agents John Thomas Downey of New Britain, Connecticut and Richard George Fecteau of Lynn, Massachusetts were shot down in northeast China while flying on a spy mission in a C-47. The United States insisted the two young men were civilians on a routine flight between Korea and Japan.

Edgar Snow, the famed American writer with long contacts and commitments in China, received a transcript of the charges against Downey and Fecteau and published them first in 1961 in his brilliant study, *The Other Side of the River.*

As excerpted from the judgment of the military tribunal of the Supreme People's Court of the People's Republic of China (November 23, 1954) the charges read: "John Thomas Downey joined the US Central Intelligence Agency, a US espionage organization in June 1951... Richard George Fecteau joined the US Central Intelligence Agency in June, 1952. Downey organized (four Chinese Nationals) into a team called 'Team Wen' and secretly air-dropped them from a US B-17 plane into Liaoning Province in September 1952. On the night of November 29, 1952 Downey and Fecteau secretly intruded into the territorial air of Northeast China in a US C-47 plane and again made contact with and provided supplies to the agents that had been air-dropped into our country. The plane in which they came, however, was shot down and Downey and Fecteau were captured. All the defendants in this case (ITALICS MINE) *have admitted the crimes committed by them after their capture.* Their crimes are also borne out by a vast amount of captured material evidence, such as weapons, ammunition, radio sets, maps, parachutes, equipment for air-dropping special agents, forged passes, certificates for wounded soldiers, as well as gold, paper currency and other instruments for conducting espionage activities...Downey personally intruded into China's territorial air to carry out criminal activities. He is the chief criminal in this case and should be punished without leniency. Fecteau who assisted Downey in intruding into China to conduct espionage activities should also be severely punished. Judgment is hereby passed: Downey is sentenced to life imprisonment and Fecteau is sentenced to 20 years imprisonment."

Fecteau was released in 1971. Downey had his sentence commuted and he was released in March of 1973.

Downey, a handsome, husky graduate of Yale, a former football player and a bright, articulate man, was recruited at college by the CIA and entered the service of The Company upon graduation. Like Redmond, he was sent to China immediately after completion of his training. Upon his release from prison in China he was retired from the service and entered Harvard Law School at age 41.

"I served my time in the prison at 13 Lane of the Grass Green Mist in Peking," he said one day while resting from his law school studies in his tasteful apartment in Cambridge. "I shared a cell with Fecteau most of the time. We could talk. Prison life through the years changed depending on conditions in the outside world. Even the food changed depending on what the political situation was at the time in China.

"The day would start with the ringing of bells and whistles at 5:30 in the morning. They would come through the cells and bang a stick on the saw horses that we slept on. The saw horses were cut low to the floor and had boards across them with a small quilt on the boards that was supposed to make it into a bed. They would bring around rice, dry bread and some salted vegetables every day and once in a while there would be a small dish of meat, a little rice and some steamed bread. We never had more than two meals a day and sometimes only one.

"There was an exercise period in the morning," Downey said, "and after that we would listen every day to the English language broadcasts on Peking radio. Three times a year they would give us some new clothes, sometimes a new Chairman Mao jacket, and take us on a tour of Peking so we could see the improvements being made in the city. My weight was two hundred and ten pounds when I was captured, went down to one hundred and eighty and then stabilized after a while at two hundred pounds. I weighed about two hundred and five now and I'm quite well considering everything.

"After Dick Fecteau was released in '71 there were still a few Chinese Nationals around who spoke English. One day we were all sitting around watching television. One of the Chinese Nationals became very animated and excited. I thought I had heard my name on the television. This guy was finally able to make it clear to me that I was being released through the kindness of the government. This was on a Sunday. The next day, Monday, I was told I was being released by prison officials. A week later they came for me and took me to the airport where I was escorted by two guards on board a plane to Canton. Then I was taken to the railroad station in Canton and two new guards traveled with me to Hong Kong. There I was let go and allowed to walk across the bridge to freedom."

Downey had never met Redmond. The only connection he had with him, really, was the visit to China made by his mother, Fecteau's mother and Redmond's mother in 1958.

"I heard his name on the Peking radio broadcast a few times," Downey said. "They always referred to him the same way. They called him 'that notorious American spy Redmond.'"

The capture of Downey and Fecteau, and their subsequent trial, conviction and sentencing, was covered thoroughly in the world press. The British news agency Reuters had a man at the trial. Back in Yonkers, the Redmonds read of the trial and wondered what this public information and trial would mean to Hugh and to them.

Late in 1951 and again early in 1952 somber-looking, conservatively dressed men identifying themselves as representatives of the United States Department of Defense visited the Redmonds at their Yonkers home. They told the Redmonds that they were working on the case and hoped to have more information soon about Hugh. They offered very little information and asked a great many questions about Hugh's past, about his service record, his friends, his political attitudes, his interests. Early in January of 1952, after Hugh's name had been revealed as a prisoner in Knowland's pronouncement, Mrs. Redmond wrote to Secretary of State Dean Acheson requesting further information on her son. She received a letter saying that information was difficult to obtain from Communist sources but indicating the United States government would keep trying. Again, in November of 1952, after hearing a brief news report on the radio that her son was dead, she wrote to Secretary Acheson.

E. J. Medill, Assistant Chief, Division of Protective Services of the State Department, wrote Mrs. Redmond on December 22, 1952:

"The Department does not appear to have received credible reports which would indicate that the Shanghai press carried an announcement of your son's death. The United States Consulate General in Hong Kong, which regularly monitors the Chinese press in Shanghai, has furnished us with no information to that effect."

The Korean war ended in 1953. Prisoners were exchanged. Still there was no word from Hugh Redmond, no word from the government, no word from the Chinese about him. Two new words entered the language as a result of the prisoner exchange and filled the pages of the American press. The words were "turncoat" and "brainwashing."

Early in 1954 the Redmond case took a strange twist. Mrs. Redmond and her husband, tired and aged now, had moved from the Belmont Avenue address to a small apartment on Floral Lane in Yonkers. The Belmont Avenue building had been sold and the new owners needed the Redmond apartment. They no longer required the services of the senior Redmond as a janitor.

"My father-in-law bought the building," said Mrs. Carmine Lemma, as she sat in her apartment in the old Redmond home at 65 Belmont Avenue. "We had to ask the Redmonds to leave. They were very upset. We knew their son was in China but we didn't know much else about it. They were not people who talked much and they certainly wouldn't tell us about that. They were very bitter toward us when they had to move."

One afternoon there was a knock on the door of Mrs. Lemma's apartment. Three men showed identification from their wallets. They said they were from the FBI.

"They kept asking us what we knew of Mrs. Redmond and her politics," said Mrs. Lemma. "They asked if we had known Hugh Redmond. We told them he had already gone by the time we moved in. They asked us if we thought Mrs. Redmond was a Communist sympathizer. They asked us if we thought that it was possible that Hugh Redmond had been brainwashed, if it was possible Hugh Redmond was staying on in China because he was a turncoat. I simply told them I didn't know anything about Hugh Redmond, had never met the man, knew nothing of his politics and simply couldn't help them. They kept asking the same questions over and over again."

It was not the first time nor the last time in the federal bureaucracy of the United States that one agency had no idea what another agency was doing. The Federal Bureau of Investigation had no idea that the man they were seeking information about, Hugh Redmond, had been sent to China not as a businessman, but as an agent of the CIA.

For some years that lack of information would make things extremely difficult for Mrs. Redmond as she sought information and aid in her ceaseless efforts to free her son.

Chapter 13

Unbreakable Will

In the late fall of 1953 Hugh Francis Redmond was drugged and carried unconscious to the Ward Road Prison in Shanghai from the house at 13 Kao Yu Road. He had become a burden to the Chinese.

Redmond never weakened in his resolve to defy the tortures and the harassment he underwent daily. His bodily strength was deteriorating but his spirit remained strong. He grew more testy, more sarcastic, more with-drawn as the endless questioning process continued. He argued with the guards in their own language. He went on hunger strikes that left him almost too weak to stand. His weight dropped to one hundred and twelve pounds. He would concede nothing. He was, under these intolerable cir-cumstances, still defiant.

The walled Ward Road Prison in the Yangtze Poo area of Shanghai had been built by the British as a municipal jail. It was a brick and stone structure with cement block cells, iron bars separating its sections and a small courtyard dividing the prison population from the administrative staff.

On January 3, 1954 the first American to be freed from the Ward Road Prison since the Communist takeover of Shanghai arrived in Hong Kong. His name was Arnold M. Kliehn. He was forty four years old, the son of missionary parents, who had been born in Shanghai and spent most of his life there. His parents had originally come from Santa Barbara, California. They settled in China in the early 1900s. Kliehn had been sent back to the United States to be educated at Vanderbilt University. After graduation he returned to China and in 1950 was arrested for having firearms in his house. He was sentenced to ten years as a counter revolutionary and expelled in 1954 on the promise he would never return.

He was a thin man, standing with difficulty at a lectern following his arrival, reporters crowding the room to hear the first testimony of an American released from prison in Communist China. His back was badly bent and his hands shook as he read a prepared statement. He suffered from beriberi and malnutrition and had difficulty seeing in the brilliantly lit room.

He said how glad he was to be out of China. He had promised never to return and he told the press of the intolerable situation at Ward Road Prison.

"Conditions are just terrible there," he said in a soft, cultured voice. "Most of the prisoners are beaten daily. Everyone must sleep on the cold floor. There is no sanitation in the cells. The cells are overrun with vermin. Prisoners urinate or defecate on themselves or on the floor where they sleep. The food is all served on filthy trays with maggots climbing all over it. If prisoners complain they are stabbed. The guards are vicious."

Kliehn was asked how many people were dying in prison from such treatment.

"Prisoners are dying at the rate of about fifteen a day," he said. "Guards are always bringing in truck loads of eight to ten men each day, sometimes bayoneting them out of the trucks, the blood spilling on the sides of the vehicle, and lining them up against the walls of the prison. Then they shoot them and let their bodies lie there for the entire day."

In Yonkers, the news of the release of Arnold Kliehn passed without much notice. The Redmond family had no way of knowing where Hugh was and could find no connection between the release of a missionary's son and the imprisonment of their son. They waited in vain for more definite word from the State Department.

A little more than three months later an event took place that would have a significant impact on the Redmond family in Yonkers.

A French Roman Catholic priest by the name of Reverend Louis Curcuffe was among twenty eight passengers aboard the coastal steamer

Hupeh as it sailed out of Shanghai for Hong Kong. Reverend Curcuffe, who had been held for more than three years by the Communists, had been freed through the efforts of the International Refugee Organization. Reverend Curcuffe had been a missionary in China for more than two decades. He discussed his imprisonment with reporters at a Hong Kong press conference. He described the conditions at Ward Road Prison where he had been held. He talked of the horrible food and the intolerable lack of sanitary conditions. An American reporter stood up and asked, "Did you hear of any Americans in the prison?"

"Only one," said the missionary.

"Do you recall his name?"

"Yes," said Reverend Curcuffe, " an American businessman, from New York. I talked to him many times in the prison courtyard. Hugh Redmond, I believe his name was,."

At the end of the press conference the American reporter cornered Reverend Curcuffe. He asked for details of his communications with Redmond.

"There isn't much to say. Redmond was the only American I saw at Ward Road. We only talked casually in the yard and there were always many guards around. I have no idea why he was arrested, what he was charged with, how long his term was. I remember that he was in terrible shape. He seemed much worse off than anyone else at the prison. He was sick, very sick, very diseased. I thought he was dying," Reverend Curcuffe said.

Curcuffe told the reporter that Redmond received the worst treatment of any prisoner held at Ward Road.

"You see," he said, "he was a very stubborn man. He fought with them all the time. He would not do as they asked. He would not listen to the propaganda lectures without interrupting. He argued with the guards about food, about treatment, about everything. He had a very bad temper. He insisted he was a legitimate American businessman and he should be set free immediately. He frightened many of the guards. They beat him with sticks but he seemed never to give in to them. He was a very strong man in spirit. Very brave. I have never seen such courage."

Reverend Curcuffe recalled Redmond's desperate physical condition when he last saw him at Ward Road.

"He was being fed poorly and beaten regularly. He was very weak, suffering from malnutrition and beriberi. He could not see well. His legs and arms were swollen. He had dizzy spells and would collapse while attempting to walk in the courtyard," the priest said.

Reverend Curcuffe said he believed Redmond would never be allowed out of prison.

"He is too stubborn a man, too strong willed, too unwilling to concede anything to them. He will not sign any papers, admit any crime. That is what one must do if one is to be allowed out of a Chinese Communist prison. It is a form of face saving for the Chinese. I do not believe Redmond will do this. I believe he is too strong willed, too brave. He will die first before he signs anything. He may already be dead," said Reverend Curcuffe.

Although the news about Redmond was horrible it was greeted with relief, almost with joy back home in Yonkers.

"These were the first words from anyone that he was still alive," said Ruth Boyle. "Until that time, we had no idea if he was alive or dead and no idea what had really happened to him. We were upset that he was sick but we felt certain he would recover if we could get him out soon. My mother immediately wrote another letter to the State Department. She seemed elated by the news. She had confidence he would recover his health if only she could get him home."

Reporters called the Redmond home after the story broke on the wires that Hugh Redmond was alive, though not terribly well, in prison.

"It is with great relief that we learned that our son, Hugh, is alive. We are hoping the Chinese will see fit to release him soon and send him back to us," Mrs. Redmond said.

Mrs. Redmond had been visited by FBI agents, representatives of the State Department and the Department of Defense on several occasions in late 1953 and 1954. She was reminded always to give people inquiring about the case the same answers she had given in the past.

"My son Hugh went to China in 1946 to work for an import-export firm," she would say. "He has been there ever since. He is a legitimate businessman and we have no idea why he is being held."

Incredibly, though neighbors and friends knew Hugh worked for the government, though tellers at the bank cashing Hugh's salary checks for Mrs. Redmond knew, though many dozens of people in and around Yonkers knew Hugh worked for the government, this cover story stood up for years.

Hugh Francis Redmond was being held by the Chinese Communists because he was an agent of the Central Intelligence Agency, an American spy. It was an admission the Chinese wanted badly from him. They could not squeeze that admission out of Redmond despite starvation, torture, disease and brainwashing attempts. Nor could anyone squeeze any information on the subject out of his small, bespectacled, ninety-eight pound mother. Hugh Redmond was a tough fellow, but there was no question where that toughness came from. Ruth Redmond was every bit as tough minded as her son.

On the morning of September 12, 1954, after more than three years of being held incommunicado, after more than three years of solitary confinement under intolerable conditions, Hugh Francis Redmond, worn, sick, weak, was marched, his hands and feet in chains, to an open square in Shanghai. There, more than two thousand residents of the city had been ordered to gather. A large table was set up in the square. Seven dour men sat at small benches behind the table. Representatives of the press of the People's Republic of China sat on a back bench. Their report of the trial would be read later that day in English on the Peking radio, monitored in Tokyo and Hong Kong, and distributed throughout the world.

Charges against Hugh Francis Redmond and seven Chinese Nationals — Wang Ko-yi, Lo Shih-hsiang, Chi Yu-kan, Ni Ching-chung, Wu Wei-fan, Hsu Pin and Huang Huang — were read to the crowd. They were all described as Nationalist agents of the United States.

"Most of the eight United States agents entered espionage service as professional spies before the liberation of China. After the liberation they used Shanghai as a center to collect state secrets, set up radio transmitters, illegally store weapons, send information to United States agents in

Hong Kong and carry out activities aimed at undermining the People's Democratic rule," the charges stated.

"Redmond, who was dispatched to China in August of 1946," the charges continued, "was engaged in espionage in Mukden, Peking and Shanghai. After the liberation of Shanghai he was ordered by the Eternal Survey Detachment 44 (a U.S. Spy group) to stay in Shanghai to maintain contact with United States intelligence organizations in Hong Kong. Under cover as an employee of the Henningsen Produce Company, a United States business establishment, Redmond directed Wang Ko-yi and other espionage teams to collect Chinese state secrets and illegally store armaments."

The Chinese said five radio sets and sixteen secret code books were recovered from the Chinese Nationalists. None were recovered from Redmond.

The trial lasted twenty two minutes. Sentences were passed quickly. Death for Wang Ko-yi. Death for Lo Shih-hsiang. Life in prison for Hugh Francis Redmond. Life in prison for Chi Yu-Kan. Life in prison for Ni Ching-chung. Fourteen years in prison for Wu Wei-fan. Fourteen years in prison for Hsu Pin. Seven years in prison for Huang Huang.

The crowd, upon hearing the expected sentences, began shouting, "KILL, KILL, KILL, KILL THE COUNTER REVOLUTIONARIES." Guards closed in on Wang Ko-yi. They dragged him through the crowd, cleared a path, leaned him against a fence and shot him to death on the spot. The senior judge then held up his hand. He announced that the death sentence against Lo Shih-hsiang was ordered suspended, pending further investigation.

In chains, almost too weak to walk or talk, Hugh Redmond was marched back to his cell in the Ward Road Prison. He had already been a prisoner of the Chinese for one thousand two hundred and forty eight days. He was now to begin a life sentence.

News of the trial and the sentence of life in prison came as a terrible shock to the Redmond family. After hearing in April through the French priest, Reverend Curcuffe, that Hugh was alive, their spirits had been lifted immeasurably. They were certain he would survive and assumed he would be freed shortly as all others seemed to be freed after serving three, four or five years in Chinese prisons. The Korean war was over, the French war in Indo-China was drawing to a close and indications of better relations between the Chinese and the United States seemed a distinct possibility.

"We are terribly bewildered by this development," Mrs. Redmond said in an interview. "We thought he would be allowed to go home. We were relieved in April when we heard the news of Hugh being alive. Now this. Where did we go from here? Of course, we would never give up but we just don't know what to do next."

In Washington the next day, at a State Department briefing, Lincoln White, the spokesman for the department rejected Chinese Communist charges that Hugh Redmond was a spy and said, "He is a legitimate businessman."

He was asked if he was categorically denying the Chinese charges that Redmond was engaged in espionage. In wonderful State Departmentese, typical of what had become standard language for an institution nicknamed Foggy Bottom, White said, "I am denying those charges by implication." He refused to elaborate any further on his choice of words.

Lower level State Department officials were badgered by reporters. They were more adamant than their seniors in denying the link between Redmond and any spying activities. Probably they were telling the truth as they knew it. They simply knew nothing. CIA activities were known to but a select few of the Washington hierarchy.

"These charges are fantastic and spurious," one State Department junior officer shouted to a reporter in a hallway. "They have no basis in fact and are typical of Communist lies."

The essence of the State Department reaction seemed clear. The louder they screamed about Communist lies and spurious charges, the less heat they would be forced to take from witch-hunting anti-Communists in and out of the Department.

Observers thought the severe sentence of life in prison for Redmond was only a smoke screen for the Chinese. They had announced previously that other Americans — mostly missionaries — would soon be released. The State Department's understanding of the sentence seemed clear. They felt the Chinese sentenced Redmond severely, making an example of him, to show Communist nations around the world that the new Communist Chinese giant was just as tough as ever on America.

No one in the State Department was ready to state publicly that Redmond was indeed a spy. Things simply weren't done that way. No one would ever admit that he was a key operator in a vast China network run by the CIA at the time of his arrest. No one in government would ever admit or even articulate the thought that the sentence of life served mutual purposes for the Chinese and the Americans.

The Chinese used Redmond to serve notice of their toughness to their own people, to increase their national pride and their anti-Americanism, to allay the fears of Communists around the world that any softening of Chinese attitudes toward America was an illusion.

The United States government was not unduly concerned. Hugh Redmond simply knew too much about a system that, at this time and for many years to come, would be beyond the awareness of most Americans. The CIA did not begin to comprehend the depth of Redmond's intense loyalty, devotion to the cause and patriotism. They simply were concerned that if he were freed, there was a possibility that an incredible amount of secret information would come to light as a result.

No one could say, probably no one in Washington really knew, that Hugh Francis Redmond was giving the Chinese a very tough time, that he fought them every inch of the way, that he was loyal to his cause, that he was, in the vernacular of sports, the toughest son of a bitch pound for pound the Chinese had ever run across.

Chapter 14

A Mother's Courage

The French were leaving Indo-China. A negotiated settlement had been achieved at Geneva. Names of strange sounding countries like North and South Vietnam, Laos and Cambodia began creeping into the American press. Lower level American and Chinese officials would actually meet across a table in Geneva. A slight thaw in the relationship between Communist China and the United States could be felt. There was no hint of recognition, nor any significant strides toward normalization, no possibility that Secretary of State John Foster Dulles would refer to that Asian giant as anything but "Communist China," but officials of the Democratic People's Republic of China did welcome new international contacts. Some book stores in Western Europe put on sale a small red covered notebook-sized volume called *Sayings of Chairman Mao*.

Late in 1954 and in the early days of 1955 there were some small changes for the better at the Ward Road Prison for Hugh Redmond

The food improved dramatically. Sanitary conditions were better. Redmond was issued clean clothes. Interrogations ceased completely. Propaganda lectures continued but were less strident in tone, and the guards seemed more humane in their attitudes. The best news for Redmond came when a guard told him he could get two books a week out of the prison library. Redmond chose a Mandarin dictionary to help him read the papers, which were always available in Chinese, and *War and Peace*.

"I was down the hall from him," remembers Father McCormack. "I used to hear thump, thump, thump all day long from his cell. In the beginning I had no idea what it was. Then one of the guards told me. Redmond was now allowed books. He read all of the books standing up. He walked up and down his cell as a form of exercise while he read, since he was not allowed outside every day as the rest of us were. The thumping noises were his shoes pounding against the floor. That man was wearing out more shoes in prison than the rest of the inmates combined."

Redmond had learned speed reading as a young man and now he was racing through every book in the prison library. Soon the Chinese relaxed the quota and he could read as many books as he liked. He became compulsive about his reading. He read almost every waking hour. A small table was finally set up in his cell. Now he could read sitting down as well as standing up. He began teaching himself other languages and he practiced reading in those languages. He mastered Mandarin Chinese and could read Chinese novels. He improved his high school Spanish and read books in that language. He started working on French and quickly became fluent. He studied Russian, had more difficulty with that language, but eventually was tackling the Russian masters in their own language.

"I remember one day he was allowed out in the courtyard," said Father McCormack. "I asked him how he was doing with his reading. 'Wonderful, Father,' he told me. 'I can't decide if I will teach French literature or Russian literature after I get home.' The reading had become the most vital part of his life. It even helped change his attitude. Now he seemed more optimistic, more hopeful that he would be freed and could go home."

Good news was also transmitted to the Redmond family in Yonkers. The State Department told them that a Chinese representative in Geneva had stated casually that letters to American prisoners in Chinese jails would be accepted. The Redmonds began writing to Hugh immediately. None of their letters were answered by him. But none were returned either. Mrs. Redmond wrote to the State Department asking if there was any way of getting the Chinese to allow her son to write back to them.

"Several relatives of the unfortunate people in this country have reported recently that prisoners are being allowed to reply to letters addressed to them," Walter J. Marx of the State Department wrote Mrs. Redmond. "It is suggested you continue to write to him."

Again, Redmond was being segregated from other American prisoners, treated differently and more harshly. He had indeed received these letters from his family. He had simply not been allowed, unlike other Americans, to answer them.

Late in 1955 Mrs. Redmond received a telegram from the State Department. She learned that the Chinese would allow her to receive letters from Hugh if she forwarded $12.50 for the purchase of stamps. She was also told the Chinese were saying that after studying the merits of each case individually they would again review the sentences of imprisoned Americans.

The stamp money was quickly dispatched to the American Consulate General in Hong Kong. The Redmonds waited. A week passed, then two, then four. They were depressed again and felt they were being cruelly tortured by the Chinese.

Finally, one Saturday morning three letters arrived in the Redmond mail box. One was a phone bill. Another was a note from a friend of Mrs. Redmond's, inviting her to a luncheon. The third letter, on thin airmail paper, was marked with the return address "Red Cross Society of China." It was a letter sent from Ward Road Prison by Hugh Redmond, then on to the Chinese Red Cross and from there to Hong Kong by rail, finally going by British air carrier to San Francisco where it was forwarded again by rail to Yonkers. It was the first word from Hugh Redmond to his family in more than four and a half years.

Dear Folks,

Merry Christmas to you and a very Happy New Year, too. I suppose you will all spend the day having dinner together at Ruthie's. I hope that the children will find what they are wishing for under the tree. Little Ruthie (Ruth Boyle's daughter, also known as Ruth) *is the only one young enough to still believe in Santa Claus. Although if she is as clever as you say she is, she may already know better.*

The letter ran four paragraphs on one side of a page of lined paper. It was signed *As ever, Hugh.* There were no references to anything other than family and weather conditions. It set the tone for every letter from Hugh that followed for the next dozen years.

"We understood that he couldn't write anything about the prison or his life," Ruth Boyle says. "It was just good to have some contact with him to see his letters, to know he was well. He had been receiving our letters, even when he couldn't answer. There were so many family things we wanted to tell him about."

In a few weeks, Mrs. Redmond received a letter from the State Department advising her that packages could now be sent to Hugh. They were limited in size and content. She had to list all the items in a separate note on the outside of the package. She sent items such as coffee, jams, canned meats, writing paper, pencils, magazines and books.

Conditions may have improved for Redmond at Ward Road Prison but he was still being kept in solitary confinement, prevented, except on rare occasions, from having any contact with other prisoners, especially Americans, and still fed a bare survival diet.

"Food is often given as a reward in Chinese prisons," says Jean Pasqualini, a French-Chinese prisoner for seven years in Peking at the Green Grass Mist Lane Prison.

Pasqualini was born in Peking of a Corsican father and a Chinese mother. He was known by his father's name, Pasqualini, and by his Chinese name, Bao Ruo-wang, as he was growing up in Peking's French school. He spoke Mandarin Chinese and French as a boy and soon learned English at a Catholic boarding school in Tientsin. He inherited most of his physical characteristics from his mother, showing almost none of the physical traits of his French father.

As a young man in pre-revolutionary China, he went to work for a Western embassy. After the Communists took over he was watched closely, arrested as a subversive and sent to prison as an enemy of the people in 1957. He was released in 1964 and deported to France, the nation of his citizenship, but a country he had never seen. He went to work for an American magazine in Paris.

"When I was in prison, the food improved when one would admit crimes of one's own free will," he says. "The Communists had an interesting system of interrogation. They wouldn't question you directly. They questioned you indirectly. They already had learned what they wanted to know and then would ask you if there was anything you felt like telling them."

Pasqualini presented his captors with a hand written seven hundred page document of his life and "crimes" in China. For his troubles he was sent to a labor camp. He reveals the hardships of these camps in his stirring book, *Prisoner of Mao,* published in 1973.

"I'm sure Redmond was not treated well because he gave them trouble," Pasqualini said one day in his Paris office. "If they were satisfied with your answers they rewarded you with food. If they were not, they would take it away."

Pasqualini never met Redmond but when he was released he was sent out of China with a man named Louis Rousset, also of French-Chinese parentage.

"I knew of Redmond on Ward Road," said Rousset, who left China for retirement in the south of France. "He was kept away from the other prisoners. I don't believe I ever talked with him. He was treated even worse than the rest of us. I know they wanted him to sign a confession. I know he never did."

Although it had been many years since Pasqualini and Rousset were freed from their Communist prison camps, they were still not able to talk of their experiences without great emotional pain.

Once a prison sentence had been imposed, the Chinese adhered strictly to the length of the sentence in very few cases. They seemed more concerned with making a public point than in extending the cruelty of long prison sentences. Pasqualini was released before his sentence expired. So was Rousset. So too with Arnold Kliehn, Reverend Louis Curcuffe and most of the other foreign prisoners. Only Redmond was held in isolation. Only Redmond was denied routine privileges. Only Redmond, the "notorious American spy" would admit nothing, sign nothing and concede nothing to the Chinese as he entered his fifth year in prison.

Late in 1955 the first non-Communist Western group to visit China since the Nationalists were defeated, entered Peking. There were twenty young people from the Society of Friends in Britain allowed to tour mainland China.

"I was among them," said J. Duncan Wood, a British Quaker, who is now an official of the International Society of Friends in Geneva. "We visited with prisoners of the Communists. We did not visit Redmond. In fact, we were unaware of his presence."

As always, the Chinese kept Redmond from outside contacts. They were afraid their CIA man might say some embarrassing things. Redmond's situation in prison seemed static. Things were moving more rapidly in his behalf back home in Yonkers.

In the early spring of 1954, some three years after Redmond had been taken prisoner by the Chinese, a committee had been formed in Yonkers to work for his release. His mother had waged her campaign alone until that point. She wrote to the State Department, to her Congressman, to Senators, government officials, newsmen, to representatives of the United States at the United Nations, to foreign governments and their ambassadors. Most answered with cordial letters. They extended sympathy for her son's plight. They could do nothing.

Yonkers Mayor Kristen Kristensen decided to establish a committee of local people to explore other avenues of gaining Redmond's freedom. The committee established for the release of Redmond knew little about the problems or intrigue they were to become involved in. They also knew little of Redmond or his work. A local businessman named William Gawchik was named chairman of the committee. When Gawchik later became ill and was unable to continue in his post, the chairmanship was turned over to a local attorney named Sol Friedman.

Friedman, a husky, handsome, balding sixty two year old man with dark eyes and a warm and sympathetic smile, had long been associated with numerous charitable causes in Yonkers. He was a World War II veteran and held the rank of Lieutenant Colonel in the United States Army reserve. He remembers the day the Redmond case became a serious cause for him.

"I had been chairman of the Redmond Committee for some time," he said, as he sat at his large mahogany desk in his Yonkers office. "We had written letters and visited with some government people. Nothing was happening."

Friedman learned that the government was making a thorough investigation of his background, checking into the charities he was involved in, asking questions about him of local businessmen, studying his friends, business associates and clients, examining his work and social habits, exploring fully every aspect of his personal and professional life.

"People in town were calling me almost daily, telling me that government representatives had been around asking questions about me," Friedman said. "They wouldn't detail what agency they were from. They would flash government identification, ask if they knew me and insist it was a routine check. Everybody was certain it was income tax people. Isn't that always what it's about when the government checks up on you?"

One afternoon Friedman was sitting in his office, his reading glasses on the tip of his nose, his desk filled with papers, his back to his open office door. He heard a shuffling of feet, looked up and saw two men standing in his office. One was tall, gray haired, hatless, about fifty years old. The other man wore a felt hat, was shorter and stockier, better dressed. The shorter man spoke first.

"Mr. Friedman?"

"Yes."

"We're from the government."

They flashed identification so quickly Friedman could not read any of it. They pulled two office chairs close to Friedman and sat down.

"My name is Howard Waters and this is Richard Doherty. We're from the government. We've been doing a check on you."

"I know. I expected you. I heard you've been around town asking questions about me."

"Yes. We wanted to find out if we could trust you. You checked out completely, so we are going to level with you."

"Thank you. This has become quite mysterious."

"We are interested in helping you in the Hugh Redmond matter."

"So that's it. Are you..."

"FBI," said Doherty.

"CIA," said Waters.

Friedman sat quietly as he told the story. It was many years ago. The moment was vivid in his mind. Still, it had an ominous ring to it. A man who was known in his community to be good character, honest, patriotic, brave, with a perfect record as a loyal American all his life. Friedman still showed signs of discomfort as he sat in his office chair years after the event, recalling that conversation.

"They told me they wanted to help," Friedman continued. "They said they would do what they could to aid our committee. They said they had the same aim as ours, to get Hugh Redmond out of that Chinese prison. I told them I would do what I could to cooperate with them. They told me they would help with contacts, with money, with different pieces of advice and information. They said I was never to tell anyone where the money was coming from. They said if it came out that the government was interested in Hugh Redmond who was supposed to be simply an American businessman, it would probably destroy any chance of getting Hugh out of China safely."

Soon Redmond's name was in the papers more often. Ads were taken out seeking the names of people who had been in China and who might have known him, or known of him. Embassy contacts were fully explored. Letters were written to ambassadors in more than seventy countries seeking aid and information on Redmond. Friedman traveled to Europe and visited several Chinese embassies.

"The Chinese always treated me well," Friedman said. "I got along fine with them. I found out there is a signal they give you if they like you and want to try to help you. They will offer you a cigarette. That is the Chinese way of saying you are a friend. It breaks down the formality of the situation."

Friedman traveled to Europe at government expense. He flew regularly to Washington to meet with CIA officials and discuss progress in the

Redmond case. The meetings were often held in black limousines with shades drawn over the windows. Sometimes money was passed to him in blank envelopes without a single word being exchanged. The money never was accounted for and never was paid in any denomination larger than a one hundred dollar bill. Every tactic was tried. The agency approved a letter writing campaign directly to Chairman Mao, and more than a thousand letters were sent to China by individuals and organizations on behalf of Redmond. Direct phone calls were made to Chinese officials in Peking. Ads were taken out in papers around the world imploring the Chinese to release Redmond. Nothing worked.

"There would be days of great hope, and other days of desperate disappointment," said Friedman. "We continued to try every avenue we could. Mrs. Redmond held up remarkably well under all this. She was an incredible woman, brave, strong, and very tough. I think of her often now and I am almost brought to tears. We tried so hard for her."

Letters were being exchanged regularly at the rate of one a month in the latter half of 1956. Hugh Redmond was now in his sixth year as a prisoner. He had still not told the Chinese anything they really wanted to hear. They had not given up trying, thought it was with very little hope of success. Redmond passed the time reading and studying almost constantly.

Shortly before Christmas, 1956, a letter arrived from Hugh at the Redmond home in Yonkers. Hugh's handwriting had changed. There was a shakiness to it.

> *My eyes have been bothering me,"* he wrote. *"I am due for an eye examination. I hope I can visit with the doctor soon and hope he may be able to help me.*
>
> *It snowed yesterday. I looked up at the sky and I let the flakes fall softly on my nose during my exercise period. It was a wonderful sensation. I enjoyed the sweet, cold touch of snow on my face. I miss you all so much. I am hoping some day soon we can be together again.*
>
> *As ever,*
>
> *Hugh*

Yonkers was hit with a heavy snow storm the day the letter arrived.

Mrs. Redmond read the letter and then went to her room. Ruth Boyle remembers that she stayed there a long time before finally coming out. It was the first time ever that Ruth could remember that her eyes were red with tears. She seemed to be aging daily. Mother and daughter fell into each other's arms and sobbed hysterically for a long while. Then, without words, they pulled apart, wiped their tears and began to prepare dinner.

Their son and brother ate a bowl of rice and drank a cup of tea in his cold, damp prison cell in Shanghai, China.

Chapter 15

Purity of Patriotism

Hugh Redmond had been having trouble with his teeth for some time. In the early days of 1957, the constant aching in his mouth grew more severe. He asked if he could see a dentist. He was taken to the Ward Road Prison hospital, examined by a female dentist and measured for false teeth. In January he wrote home about the problem.

> *Dear Folks,*
>
> *I told you about my problem with my teeth last month. The pain was more intense late in December. I was examined earlier this month. Most of my teeth were pulled. The new teeth were made and I have been trying them out. They did a fine job and I am sure I will get used to them after a while. The important thing is there is no more pain.*
>
> *Your September and October letters arrived together. I also received copies of Sport Magazine for those months. I could hardly believe the story about Jackie Robinson being traded to the hated Giants. What is this world coming to anyway? It would be so wonderful if I could be home in time for the next World Series.*
>
> *As ever,*
>
> *Hugh*

In Yonkers, Mrs. Redmond was carefully following a series of articles being printed each day in the *New York Post*. They were written by a young Negro journalist named William Worthy Jr. Worthy was then traveling in Communist China. He would learn a great deal about how China worked, how the United States State Department worked, how firm were the United States attitudes toward China and how muddled was the American bureaucracy. He would also bring back valuable information about Hugh Redmond.

Some two years earlier, in 1955, Worthy began thinking seriously of an unusual trip. As a graduate student at Harvard, thirty three years old, he was interested in journalism and broadcasting, and immersed in Negro causes. He was anxious to see first hand how the Communist states of Russia and China dealt with American Negroes, how the continent of Africa was awakening to its revolutionary movement and new black awareness. He planned to take trips to Russia, Africa and China.

A Negro newspaper in Baltimore called the *Afro-American* and several other liberal newspapers, notably the *New York Post*, together with some radio stations, agreed to underwrite the costs of his trip. Worthy visited Russia and Africa and hoped to become the first American newsman allowed into China since the Communists claimed the country in 1949.

The trips to Russia and Africa went off well. His articles were bright and enlightening. They made small impact, however, since many American newsmen had traveled extensively in both areas for years. China was another matter.

Worthy applied for a visa to China. He heard nothing. Neither the Chinese government nor the United States government took much notice of the impending trip. No American newsman had been allowed inside China since their revolution and the situation seemed unlikely to change now.

On December 16, 1956, Worthy received a cablegram from Chu Lieh, secretary of the information department of the Chinese Foreign Ministry. It read:

> *YOUR APPLICATION TO VISIT CHINA GRANTED. ONE MONTH VISA TO BE COLLECTED AT SUM-CHON BEFORE DECEMBER 31. TRAVEL AT OWN EXPENSE. CONTACT CANTON BRANCH, CHINESE INTOURIST FOR ACCOMMODATIONS.*

Worthy was overjoyed at the chance to examine the Chinese revolution first hand, to make journalistic history and to gain an insight into Communist thought as it pertained to Americans in general and Negro Americans in particular.

He was given two major assignments by the *Afro-American,* the *New York Post* and the Columbia Broadcasting System, which now signed on as a sponsor for the trip. They wanted interviews with American prisoners of war captured by the Chinese and North Koreans and held in China despite the supposed total exchange of prisoners after the Korean armistice. They also wanted interviews with so-called American "turncoats," those veterans of the Korean conflict who had decided to stay on in China voluntarily after the Korean war had ended. Most of these men, it was assumed, had been "brainwashed" with Communist dogma.

Hugh Redmond fell into the former category.

Worthy left New York in early January, flew out of Idlewild airport for Seattle, boarded a Pan American flight for Tokyo and flew a Japan Airlines plane into Hong Kong. There he boarded a train and arrived for a two day stay in Canton. He flew on to Peking where he interviewed Chinese leaders. Arrangements were made for him to interview, for the first time for an American audience, these "turncoats." He also asked for permission to interview the American businessman sentenced as a spy, Hugh Francis Redmond. He was told Redmond was "unavailable for interviews." He discussed Redmond's case with Chinese officials. They were vague. They told Worthy, "The notorious American spy Redmond could not be seen." Worthy would have to take their word that he was well.

A few days after he arrived in China, Worthy was allowed to interview a former GI by the name of William C. White of Morriltown, Arkansas. The interview appeared in the *New York Post,* the *Afro-American* and was broadcast on CBS.

"Many émigré colored Americans," Worthy wrote, "fed up with stateside Jim Crowism have made happy cultural adjustments amidst the loneliness of Paris or Rome.

"Former Corporal William C. White and two of his friends are unique in having sought racial asylum in a backward country where refrigerators, bathtubs and automobiles are few and far between.

" 'To confuse the American people,' White told me in his room at People's University, where he has begun the study of law, 'the United States government said we were brainwashed. If being brainwashed is wanting peace, equality and an end to all unjust and fascist systems, then I've been brainwashed and I brainwashed myself. Others didn't do it. I stayed behind because I wanted to. There was no force. The Chinese didn't offer me any big mansion or any pretty Chinese girl.' "

Worthy continued his report. "However these words may read in print they were spoken without a trace of bitterness or hostility. White's comments on political and racial topics do not make the listener feel he is hearing original thought and analysis. Rather the remarks are more like mechanical playbacks of lectures and indoctrination, spoken in practically neutral tones as if from memory. Communism was not entirely new to Corporal White in August 1950 when he arrived in Korea to fight Communism. While serving in the Army in Seattle he had mixed socially with colored Communists. 'I was not a Communist,' he says, 'but I wanted to know what Communism was.'

"To hard-pressed American Communists, the self-appointed champions of oppressed minorities, the young kid in military uniform must have come as a welcome potential recruit in the lean cold war days of 1949. From that standpoint he had the advantage of being unmistakably colored. Way back in the thirties, light brown-skinned Angelo Herndon began to sour on his comrades when he overheard a white Communist remark, 'It's too bad he isn't blacker.' But Corporal White is quite dark in complexion and in terms of physique and height, he fits into the category that white girls at left wing parties and social gatherings snuggle up to and make a fuss over."

Worthy's report continues, "The first time I saw him at the university he was wearing a blue pencil-stripe suit, black shoes and brown shirt with no tie. When he ventured out into the cold night he put on a jacket that apparently made up in warmth for all that it lacked in style. His suit, too, while serviceable, could easily be matched in any third or fourth rate store on, say, Chicago's South Side where marginal customers make small down payments on unattractive goods and meet their subsequent installments whenever The Man catches them.

"This most important decision in White's life was not a hasty one. 'It took a lot of consideration and it was all a decision of my own.' He said he followed the truce talks at Panmunjom and saw the proposals put forward by both sides and analyzed them, and saw which side really wanted peace. 'I examined why the United States was in Korea and the things U. S. troops did in Korea. We saw U. S. planes bombing peaceful villages, not just military targets. In South Korea they were raping the women. So all of these things began to add up. This caused you to think. Why should we have war? Who starts war?'

"Corporal White of course had a ready at-hand interpretation of the how's and why's of racial discrimination. 'Discrimination is a product of the Capitalist system. The only way for us colored people to have equality is to have a system like the Chinese system.' "

Reports of Worthy's interviews and many of his comments were being heard in China, especially some of what he had discussed with Corporal White, who was well known throughout China as one of the Americans who had stayed behind.

Father McCormack remembers meeting Hugh Redmond in the exercise area of Ward Road Prison one afternoon during the tour by Worthy. He asked Redmond if he had heard any of the newsman's comments on the prison radio. "He looked at me, made a sour face and he said, 'Crap.' Then he walked away," said Father McCormack. General McAuliffe would have understood that comment coming from one of his paratroopers.

It was clear that Hugh Redmond had not been brainwashed.

It was also clear from a careful reading of all of Worthy's interviews, essays and discussions, that he had not been brainwashed either. He painted an accurate picture of life in China for most of these Americans, portraying their problems and confusion and making clear he saw nothing very wonderful about their new lives, even though their old lives were far from perfect. He also did an accurate job of portraying life in China for the Chinese. He complimented them on the cleanliness of their streets, the personal involvement of the people in the running of their cities and the dedication of their leaders to Chairman Mao and his ideals. Worthy was a fine reporter. Nothing else.

The United States State Department, still dominated by John Foster Dulles' doctrinaire attitudes, saw Worthy's trip in a different light. They reasoned that China was a Communist country and any man who visited a Communist country must therefore, be a Communist. When Worthy returned to the United States he was immediately stopped by representatives of the Department of Justice and agents of the Immigration and Naturalization Service. His passport was examined and finally confiscated. Worthy's right to travel freely as an American citizen had been denied him, without due process. The State Department simply said that he had violated the ban on travel to Communist China. This seemed like utter nonsense since the State Department had granted the passport in the first place, with prior knowledge that Worthy planned to enter China. The government simply decided to intimidate him and the press organizations who supported him by picking up his passport.

In Yonkers, Sol Friedman and the Committee to Free Hugh Redmond immediately contacted Worthy. They asked if he had seen Redmond. He told them he had not. He told them he had heard of him from Chinese officials. He suggested ways to Mrs. Redmond and the Committee for approaching the Chinese on the Redmond case.

Worthy's trip and his subsequent troubles with the State Department made headlines across the country. It focused attention on a sore point among many Americans, the country's stiff attitude toward the Chinese. Americans could travel extensively through Communist Russia, but because there was no recognition of Communist China, no travel at all was to be allowed to that country. It seemed illogical. What was the United States afraid of, if Worthy and other newsmen were not allowed to travel freely to China?

Many Americans were curious about Worthy's trip. People seemed sincerely concerned about the Americans who stayed behind in China after the Korean War ended. There was an air of mystery about many of these men and Worthy's articles had done much to clear it up. Who were these Americans? Why did they stay? Were there any more like them? What were their true reasons for turning their backs on their American homes and families, on the American system and traditions, for a place in China? The curtain of mystery surrounding these men seemed to cast doubts about ourselves and our values.

In the spring of 1957, as Hugh Redmond entered his seventh year as a prisoner of the Chinese, the Committee on Foreign Affairs of the House of Representatives, Eighty-Fifth Congress, decided to examine the questions involving these men. The Subcommittee on the Far East and the Pacific would examine the entire question of American prisoners in hearings to be held in several cities on the East coast, including New York, Baltimore and Washington, with special emphasis on the approximately four hundred and fifty Americans who had been held as prisoners of war and had not been accounted for by the Communists. Most of these men were considered "turncoats."

The Committee was under the chairmanship of Congressman Clement J. Zablocki. One of its members included a young Congressman from Ohio by the name of Wayne Hays, whose name would fill the newspapers across the country in connection with activities involving a Miss Elizabeth Ray some twenty years later.

One of the witnesses called before the Committee was William Worthy. He described his trip to China. He explained that he had made specific requests for information on American prisoners from the Chinese and through the British, who represented American interests there. He detailed how difficult it was to get any information from Chinese Communist sources on the Americans. He related much of the communications he had with American families seeking information on their sons, husbands and brothers still in China some four years after the Korean War had ended.

" Mr. Chairman, one mother in New Jersey who I interviewed got in touch with me," Worthy said. "All of these people have come to me. I had no way of getting in touch with them. They have either phoned, wired or written me. This mother in New Jersey said something like this: 'I lie awake at night composing strong letters to the State Department. Then I never send them because I am afraid the State Department will call me a Communist.'

"I said to her, 'What if they do? You are interested in getting your son back.'

"She said, 'Yes, but I don't want to raise that much trouble in Washington.'

"All of these people who have contacted me seem for some reason or other to tremble when they come to Washington and try to deal with officials. They are definitely on the defensive in dealing with these agencies."

Worthy went on to explain how he had interviewed the Reverend Paul J. Mackensen of Baltimore, a Lutheran missionary who had been in China for nine years. He interviewed Mackensen in the Ward Road Prison, the same prison in which Redmond was being held. Worthy had never been allowed to see Redmond. After interviewing Mackensen at Ward Road he concluded that the Reverend from Baltimore had been brainwashed.

"The condition of Reverend Mackensen," Worthy told the Committee, "was pathetic, not so much in terms of physical conditions. The jail was unheated. He sat through the interview with his hands in his sleeves because he had no gloves. The place gave you complete moral and spiritual chills, quite aside from physical chills. There were two prison personnel sitting in on the interview, both of whom spoke English. He gave me a definite impression of having been converted to the Communist system. He praised his jailers and praised the achievements of the Communist regime during the last eight years in power. I understand from other sources he had definite guilt feelings, was made to believe that he was guilty as a missionary of having served the West, of having spied for the West. Now he feels he must go through penance and he wants to stay there and serve the Chinese people under the Communist regime."

Worthy then explained that he had contacts after he got back to the

United States with mothers of other prisoners in China. Meanwhile, Mackensen, obviously brainwashed, was the only prisoner he was allowed to see. Any other Americans he had been able to talk with while he was in China were all supposedly free men.

"One mother," he continued in his talk before the Committee, "Mrs. Redmond of Yonkers, New York, mother of Hugh Redmond who was in the same Shanghai jail, asked me to meet with her and two or three members of her Committee to free Hugh Redmond in Yonkers."

Worthy explained that he had also been contacted by the mothers of John Downey and Richard Fecteau. They had communicated often and regularly from the start of their imprisonment with their families. Worthy knew that Redmond had never been allowed such privileges, that the American businessman was allowed rare communication and then only after nearly five years of silence.

"There seems no rhyme or reason to the Communist treatment of prisoners. One is allowed to write regularly and another has been allowed to send only three letters during six years of imprisonment," Worthy said.

Worthy had no way of knowing that Hugh Redmond, the "notorious American spy," would not talk, would not sign anything, would not cooperate with his captives — that Redmond alone lived up fully to what he accepted as his oath of loyalty and morality when he joined the CIA. Redmond's case was different, by God, because Hugh Francis Redmond was different.

Worthy continued to detail his meetings and conversations with the Redmond committee. He explained how they had attempted a letter writing campaign and how they were discouraged from completing it by representatives of the State Department, how they had always run into a stone wall when they asked for official government help, how they had prepared a list of civic organizations backing their requests and were prevented from meeting with President Eisenhower and getting a hearing on their cause, how they had forwarded a list of these civic organizations supporting their cause to Mao Tse-tung instead of President Eisenhower because they felt that the Chinese leader might actually be more sympathetic to their quest than their own American President.

In a sharp exchange, Congressman Hays chastised Congressman Zablocki for criticizing the Redmond Committee for sending the list to Mao instead of to Eisenhower. It was Zablocki's reasoning that this naturally made all of the Redmond Committee members Communists. Hays said he didn't believe that was so.

"I think the whole thing is that they are worked up emotionally," said Congressman Hays, "and that they are not going to be satisfied with anything the State Department does, however reasonable it may be, until they produce their son."

For the Redmonds the appearance of William Worthy at the hearings had created some publicity, made more people aware of Hugh's plight, antagonized some State Department and Congressional officials but had contributed little to their main cause. It did not bring Hugh Redmond any closer to home.

After the hearings the Committee to Free Hugh Redmond was encouraged to send more letters to China, to make public appeals for help, ask more foreign nations to explore their conduits with China, working to explore every avenue for Redmond's release.

Another letter arrived from Hugh in the summer of 1957. He reported that he was well. His false teeth were comfortable, he had put some weight on, and he continued hoping that he would soon be coming home.

It is my hope that I will no longer have to write you by this time next year. I can only hope that whatever we have to say to each other we can say in person. For now I am reading as much as I can. I have started reading Chinese novels. My dictionary is out of date. See if the latest Mathews English-Chinese dictionary is available in New York.

P.S. Ice cream for the children.

As ever,

Hugh

In the summer of 1957 a World Youth Festival, sponsored by left wing organizations, had been held in Moscow. Many American students attended. Some were leftists, others were simply curious young men and women, anxious to get a look at Russia and see the Communist system at work for themselves. In the midst of the trip, a Chinese official approached one of the leaders, the Reverend John McKenna of Boston, forever after to be known as the Red Priest.

"Would you like to visit China on the way home?"

It was an intriguing idea. Despite the ban on travel to Communist China that still existed after Worthy's earlier trip, some twenty young men and women, mostly students, went to China. They were allowed to visit with Americans in Chinese jails in groups of twos and threes. One group visited John Downey and Richard Fecteau in Peking. They were greeted warmly by the two CIA agents who had been shot down over China. Another group visited Hugh Redmond in Shanghai. They were able to speak with Father McCormack and the Reverend John Wagner of Pittsburgh, also being held at Ward Road Prison.

Steve and Pat Tyler, two young American students, were escorted into the prison waiting room. In a few minutes, Redmond, looking suspicious, arrived from his cell. Only five minutes before, he had been informed that two young American students wished to talk to him. He had not spoken to any Americans except, occasionally, to his fellow prisoners in more than six years. He was very suspicious, and treated the Tylers with hostility and coldness.

Redmond said he knew of the ban on travel to China by Americans. He could not understand. How had the Tylers come to China? They tried to explain. He was sarcastic about their having visited Russia. They asked about his attitudes toward his Communist captors.

"I am an anarchist," he suddenly shouted at them. "I am certain you have broken the laws of the United States coming here. I don't want to see you and I don't want to break any American laws by talking to you."

The Tylers were taken aback by the passionate hostility displayed by this American but still they continued to press on with the interview as guards listened carefully. They were certain Redmond had to be what he insisted he was: an American businessman illegally imprisoned.

"Did you ever consider yourself politically conscious," Pat Tyler asked him.

"What the hell is that — a Marxist question? I have been reading a lot of Marxist books and that sounds familiar," Redmond retorted.

The Tylers could not find much common ground with Redmond. They tried to talk of things outside of politics. They discussed the weather back home, and general trivia about their school and their trip. Redmond seemed to soften somewhat as they gave him the latest news in sports. They exchanged a few more pleasantries and promised Redmond they would contact his family for him when they got home. He thanked them for that. Then he was led away. The entire discussion had taken less than five minutes.

The Tylers returned to New York and were interviewed when they arrived back home. They were asked about Redmond.

"He's one hundred per cent American," Steve Tyler said, "and hard as nails."

In Yonkers, Mrs. Redmond was pleased to hear that Hugh seemed well, looking even younger, according to the Tylers, than his years would indicate, and absolutely steadfast in his attitude toward his country.

"I am certainly pleased and not surprised," said Ruth Redmond, "that Hugh has remained fanatically American."

If the Chinese were still trying to break Hugh Redmond, if they were still trying to get him to sign a statement, admit his CIA connections, apologize for his actions, they were in for a tough battle.

More than eleven years had now passed since Hugh Redmond had been in America, more than six years had passed since he had been taken prisoner by the Chinese Communists. One thing remained constant.

Hugh Francis Redmond was filled with an old fashioned, out of date, much-maligned virtue known as patriotism.

Chapter 16

Mrs. Redmond's Trip to China

On December 5, 1957 the United States State Department sent identical telegrams to the families of Hugh Redmond, John Downey and Richard Fecteau.

BAN ON TRAVEL TO COMMUNIST CHINA IS HERE-
BY LIFTED IN YOUR INDIVIDUAL CASE. YOU MAY
APPLY FOR VISA FORTHWITH FOR EXTENDED
STAY. FURTHER DETAILS FOLLOW BY MAIL.

"When my mother got that telegram," says Ruth Boyle, "she was determined to go to China and come back home with my brother. She was certain she could do it."

William Worthy's trip to China had opened a crack in the Bamboo Curtain. The trip to China by the students from the World Youth Festival had opened it even wider. Now three middle aged mothers, all longing for their sons, would come rushing through that opening.

Ruth Redmond, sixty years old, slight of build and with bad eyesight, cabled foreign minister Chou En-lai for permission to enter China and visit her son on December 14, 1957. Three days later she received a cable from China telling her that she would be able to pick up a visa good for two weeks travel inside China.

Similar requests were made by Mrs. Downey and Mrs. Fecteau. The three mothers decided to begin their journey together from Idlewild Airport in New York at noon on January 1, 1958. The hours before their trip passed slowly.

"I hope the Reds haven't changed my son too much," Mrs.

Redmond told a reporter in an interview shortly before the trip. "But even if they have it won't make any difference. He is still my boy and I love him."

Mrs. Redmond confessed that the trip was not without serious difficulty.

"Ever since I received permission from Chou En-lai to visit my son, people have been asking me if I'm not scared to be heading for China. But I'm not. Maybe I should be but I guess my mother love is stronger than my fear. I can't let myself think of the reason behind my invitation anyway. I just want to see Hugh," she said.

Plans for the trip went forward. The Hugh Redmond Committee in Yonkers raised the fourteen hundred dollars necessary for expenses. Mrs. Redmond was given a leave of absence with pay from her job as a cafeteria manager by the Yonkers Board of Education. Her husband, tired and ailing now, would stay behind and be cared for by his daughter.

"After all of my fruitless attempts for permission to visit my son, it is hard to believe my dream is about to come true," she said. "This will be the happiest New Year's Day of my life."

"I am very concerned with Hugh's reaction," she continued. "Will he be expecting me? Will they tell him?" I hope the shock won't be too much for him. That's the thought that has haunted me for two weeks."

There was one other thought that Mrs. Redmond expressed in the newspaper interview.

"What does a mother say to a son she hasn't seen in over eleven years? And after my two weeks are up, how will I ever say good-bye to him?"

The Chinese had made clear during talks through third parties in Geneva and Warsaw as early as 1955 that the mothers of American prisoners would be welcomed in China. It was the United States government that had kept the mothers out. Now there was a growing fear in the Eisenhower administration that the mothers would embarrass the United States somehow, that their statements would be turned into useful Communist propaganda, that the Chinese would be using them to make political points, especially with that segment of the American population without the same violent anti-Communistic attitudes articulated by John Foster Dulles. All statements made by the mothers to the press before the trip were carefully studied. The State Department assigned a low level official to give them a briefing on what they might expect. The briefing sounded very much like military orders of conduct.

With reporters and photographers in attendance, with television cameras and microphones everywhere, with officials of the government, the Yonkers committee and the airlines in attendance, the three mothers and a brother of John Downey boarded a United Airlines flight out of Idlewild for San Francisco. There they would change to a British Overseas airliner for the long flight to Hong Kong.

In Shanghai, Hugh Redmond had been told of the trip by prison officials.

"He was happy," Father McCormack remembers, "but he wasn't one to be carried away. He was a stoic. This was not a boy who was given to much emotion. Even upon seeing his mother."

Ruth Boyle remembers her mother describing that first moment together with Hugh after eleven long years.

"She told me there were no tears, not from her, not from Hugh, very little emotion. They were both affected by the realization that Hugh was still in prison, still subject to all that pressure. He was not being freed. It was a welcome visit for both of them, but neither Hugh nor my mother could know if there would be another visit. My mother wasn't a woman given much to tears," says Ruth Boyle. "Neither was my brother. They kept everything inside them."

Since the trip was paid for by the Redmond committee and since Yonkers' interest in the journey was enormous, Mrs. Redmond sat down when she returned home and wrote out in longhand a twenty page detailed account of her trip.

I visited Hugh at the Ward Road Prison, she began. *It is a huge gray building. He is in good health, weighed 145 pounds and of late had been allowed to exercise a lot and had lost some of his excess weight. Around Christmas time last year he had received excel-*

lent dental treatment and his new teeth look and felt fine.

I entered the prison through the main gate where soldiers were on guard. I met Hugh in a large plain room where the only furniture was a table and two chairs. Hugh obviously had quite a distance to come as he was dressed in a heavy overcoat since it was quite cold outside. I had seven visits with him, each lasting from two to two and a half hours. Hugh was well dressed in a business suit, blue shirt and tie and a woolen jacket. On extremely cold days he also wore a heavily padded overcoat. At my last visit with Hugh, I was asked by the Red Cross if I would like to have dinner with Hugh. I ordered a special dinner from the hotel which was brought into the room at the prison and we ate together. Upon termination of each meeting Hugh left the room first. I would remain seated and then would be escorted out of the prison.

Hugh stated that he was imprisoned at one end of the prison yard in what formerly had been a caretaker's house. He had a room in which there was a dresser, bed, desk and chair. The bathroom was at the end of the hall and he was allowed one bath a week. At the other end of the hall was a room in which Father McCormack was imprisoned. I had brought a message from Father McCormack's sister, a nun, Sister Oona. I was not permitted to talk to Father McCormack but an interpreter said he would deliver the message to Father McCormack.

After my first visit to Hugh I shopped for food and fruits at the market and these were all given to Hugh. On one occasion, Hugh indicated that for breakfast he was given Chinese mush, tea and bread. He depended on Red Cross packages for food such as meats, candies and coffee. He said he did not have enough to read. I com-

plained about that to the Red Cross escort and prior to my leaving, Hugh did receive more reading material from the Red Cross.

Most of our conversations related to family affairs, Hugh's old friends and general conditions in the United States. He said he could write home every month though some of his letters were not received. He said he could purchase certain things such as fruit and vegetables if he had money so I left one hundred and fifty dollars with him. From my conversations at the prison with Hugh I felt certain that he was not getting all the items I sent him. Later I saw evidence of this.

The trip over was pleasant but extremely long and tiresome. We stayed in Hong Kong for several days before we were told we could enter China. Upon leaving Hong Kong we crossed the bridge into Red China on foot and were escorted by Chinese officials. Chinese soldiers took our passports and immediately indicated the passports were no good. This frightened all of us since we thought we had made the long trip for nothing. Later we found out the Chinese were using the passports in order to make propaganda about the failure of the United States to recognize the People's Republic of China. The Communists took exception to the use of 'Communist China' on our documents.

We went from Hong Kong by train to Canton. There we stayed at the Oi Kuen Hotel. It was at this point that Mrs. Downey and Mrs. Fecteau flew on to Peking to visit their sons and arrangements were made for my onward travel to Shanghai to see Hugh.

On the morning of 8 January 1958, at 6:15 A.M. I left Canton by plane for Shanghai. I flew in a small two-engine plane in which there was a cargo of oranges. There was only one other passenger, a Chinese woman who was carrying a large bunch of green bananas. It was an eight hour flight and there was one stop at Nanchang. I could not even get a glass of water on the plane and there were no toilet facilities. There was room for only two passengers since there was only one double seat on one side of the plane. There were no safety belts and it was a very cold and miserable trip. The Chinese woman asked me if I was cold and then gave me her blanket. She also had some hard candies which she offered to share with me. I had some Life Savers in my purse which I in turn gave to the woman. At Nanchang there was a lunch waiting for me. There was enough for several people and when it became apparent that the other woman was not getting any lunch, I offered to share it with her. The remainder of the plane trip was spent discussing the weather and incidentals. The woman indicated she had two children.

On my first visit to the prison I saw this woman in the background of the large crowd that had assembled at the prison gates. Later, this woman came to my room at the Palace Hotel and said, 'Good evening, Mrs. Redmond.' She said her name was Ling. When I asked her why she hadn't spoken to me at the prison, Mrs. Ling said she thought it best that we did not talk to each other at the prison.

My first meeting with Hugh was covered by cameras and many reporters. Mrs. Ling had identified herself as a reporter. I understood that motion pictures of this meeting were later shown in the United States.

Although I did not take a camera with me they furnished me with one when we went on tours. These tours included visits to schools, where I met the dean of the university and to private homes of the Chinese. They first took me to the old Chinese section to show me how

life was in old China. Then they took me to the new hous-
ing developments which consisted of apartments and
which the Chinese indicated they considered heaven. I
was invited to stay for dinner at these homes and on one
occasion I did accept a cup of tea.

Besides the schools I visited several factories.
Throughout the tours there was much talk of peace and
trade with the United States. I was taken to areas where
people lived in poverty and on junks on the water but was
told that soon all this would disappear. Much was made
of the fact that I was the first American to come and visit
these factories and many of the Chinese said they would
like to come to the United States and visit.

Mr. Wen, the Red Cross man, said he could not
dine in the hotel since only hotel guests are allowed to
eat there. As a result I had difficulty ordering meals
because I could not read Chinese and the menus were in
Chinese. I ended up having a cup of tea and toast at
every meal and on one occasion Mr. Wen expressed concern that I was not having enough to eat.

I could have gone on a lot more trips around
Shanghai but I quite often was too tired. I was asked if I
wanted to go to Suchow which is noted for its famous
parks. It was not until after I agreed that I found out that
it was an overnight trip. The parks were beautiful and I
visited an embroidery shop and a fan factory. The countryside between Shanghai and Suchow was rural. Later,
in Peking, when I talked to Mr. Morgan, under-secretary
of the British Embassy, he said he could not believe that
I had gone to Suchow since the British had been asking
for a long time to make the trip and they were told they
could not go.

The only time that Hugh left the room was when
the pictures were taken standing in the entrance to the

prison. The Red Cross asked if I would like to have my picture taken with Hugh, and, of course I agreed.

In Shanghai I wrote my first letter to Chou En-lai. I took this letter and mailed it myself as I did my second letter. Mr. Wen then came to me and told me that someone in authority said that I could go to Peking at my own expense and that I would meet Chou En-lai there. It was at this time that I received a week's extension of my stay. The trip to Peking was made available to me by the Red Cross and I again rode a small two engine plane. It was a very bad and bumpy trip. We traveled for eight hours leaving Shanghai at 7:30 in the morning and did not arrive until 5 o' clock that night. I was met at the airport by John Downey's brother, Bill. The Downeys were at the Peace Hotel and were escorted by Red Cross girls. They had better food at this hotel although it was not as elaborate as my Shanghai hotel. The Reuters man, Mr. Gee, had taken hundreds of pictures of the other two women and was anxious to get us all together.

Mr. Morgan met me and was very pleasant. We had a much publicized meeting with Li Teh Chuan. At the conclusion of the meeting, after pleading with this high Chinese official for the release of our sons, she stated that she had sons of her own and knew how the mothers felt and that we should not abandon hope because sometimes things change.

During my last meeting with Hugh he would not make any statements about getting out. He said he hoped it would not be twelve years before we got together again and that without a little hope one could not live. He added that I should trust the airlines and he would be seeing me soon.

Mrs. Redmond flew on to Peking after her final visit in Shanghai with her son. She met with representatives of the Chinese government, requesting her son's release on humanitarian grounds. She awaited word in a Peking hotel. She hoped that her son would be freed and they could fly home together. She received a phone call from a low level Chinese official who told her the Red Cross would soon have a statement for her about her son.

"Is he free?" she asked.

"You will hear from the Red Cross," the man said. Then he hung up.

Another two hours passed. The phone rang in her room again and the earlier caller identified himself carefully now as Chi Feng, Assistant Director for International Relations for the Chinese Red Cross. He would be over shortly to see her in her hotel room. He asked Mrs. Redmond to be waiting in her room for him with a pencil and pad. She had a pencil. She had no pad. She took a postcard from her purse and waited. Soon there was a knock.

The Director, a small man with thick glasses and a precise, clipped British way of speaking English, began, "The Premier fully understands the feelings behind your appeal. But your son has violated Chinese laws and must be dealt with accordingly. My government has a policy of leniency toward criminals who behave well while serving their terms. Any criminal who so behaves may have the opportunity for leniency. This applies to your son.

Mrs. Redmond had been instructed to write the statement down as Chi spoke. She did so in pencil on a picture post card showing the Bund in Shanghai.

"Then she came home," said Ruth Boyle. "She would look at that postcard over and over again, shake her head and say nothing. It was as if she thought by wishing she could change the words on the card to 'Your son, Hugh, may leave with you now for the United States.' "

The three mothers left Peking together without their sons for the long journey home. They flew from Peking to Canton. There they took a train to Hong Kong, had no border problems on their exit and walked across the bridge and out of Communist China.

Both Mrs. Downey and Mrs. Fecteau would each live to see their sons return home again to the United States. Mrs. Redmond would see her son on two other occasions in Ward Road Prison on trips to China in 1962 and 1963. She would never lose hope of bringing him home. She alone would carry that forlorn hope to her death.

"My mother was a remarkable woman," says Ruth Boyle. "She was very strong, very brave. I never saw her lose faith, I never saw her break down. I often wondered how she survived so much pain for so long."

There were more newspaper interviews when Mrs. Redmond returned home, more discussions for new approaches, more letters written, more contacts followed up on, more hours spent on the long, frustrating details of arranging new plans. Nothing helped. Hugh Redmond stayed behind the walls of Ward Road Prison.

In a month after her first trip to China, a letter from Hugh arrived. He commented on his mother's visit:

> *It was so good to see you again, mother and I hope you had a safe journey home. I know it was very long and tiresome and at your age (don't worry, I won't tell) you must try and take it a little easier. I have gotten many new books and have been reading a great deal since you left. Buy some ice cream for little Ruthie and the others and tell them it is from Uncle Hughie. Maybe some day soon we can be sharing ice cream together.*
>
> *As ever,*
>
> *Hugh*

Some months after she returned home in 1958, Mrs. Redmond received a cheering letter from Father McCormack. He had been released from Ward Road Prison and was now back with his order in Maryknoll, New York.

> *I remember the day I left Ward Road,* Father McCormack wrote Mrs. Redmond. *I was the last American there except for Hugh and I knew it was going to be hard for him. He had all his books and his foreign language studies and his exercises but I knew the boy would have no other Americans to talk to, not that we were ever allowed much time for idle chatter. We stood in*

the courtyard together before I left and there was nothing
either of us could say. I felt tears coming to my eyes.
Hugh smiled at me. He patted me on the shoulder. He
said how happy he was that I was finally going home
again. I knew I was leaving him behind to a fate only
God knew. I looked at him and I knew I would never see
him again. I wanted to say something helpful to him. I
could not. I was saddened, Mrs. Redmond, because I
feared so that they would never let him out. He never said
good-bye. We just turned from each other and walked
away. I shall pray for your son.

Meetings continued, often among the members of the Redmond
committee through the late days of 1958. All sorts of suggestions were
made, some possible, some incredibly wild. One member's idea was for
a sneak bombing attack on Ward Road Prison and a parachute rescue of
the veteran paratrooper. Every idea was considered. Nothing seemed fea-
sible. Hugh continued to write. Packages were sent to him, with books,
shoes and aspirin along with some tins of food as treats.

Early in 1959, Hugh Redmond's father, age seventy five, suffered a
heart seizure and died.

"We were sure," said Ruth Boyle, "that the Chinese would allow
Hugh out now as the sole surviving son of a widowed mother. They had
always been portrayed as a family people, concerned, understanding,
compassionate about their own parents. We wrote another letter to Chou
En-lai through the Chinese Red Cross. We informed them that Hugh's
father had died and asked, in the name of human compassion, for his
release."

The letter was never answered by the Chinese. Hugh's father was
buried quietly on a small plot in the Oakland Cemetery in Yonkers, New
York. Redmond's next letter home two months later made his mother and
sister aware that he had been told the news.

"I am glad that it was quick," he wrote. "It is not always so."

Hugh Redmond was forty years old now and he was slowly dying,
each day as painful as the last, each hour filled with emptiness, each

moment filled with the realization that in all likeliness he would never return home.

Don't forget the ice cream for the children, he wrote in
the letter acknowledging his father's death. *Life goes on.*
Uncle Hughie wants the children to be happy.

There was to be no happiness for Uncle Hughie as the decade of the sixties began and Redmond finished his ninth year in prison.

Chapter 17

Death of a True Believer

John Fitzgerald Kennedy, the new President of the United States, created an air of excitement in Washington, around the country and throughout the world in the early days of his administration in 1961.

Ruth Redmond sent letters to the new President, the new Secretary of State, Dean Rusk, to the new Attorney General, Robert F. Kennedy, to United States Senator Jacob Javits of New York and to scores of other United States government and other foreign officials.

Neatly typed replies, filled with official sounding words, came back through the mail. Hugh Redmond was no closer to getting out of his China prison. New York Senator Kenneth Keating called the Redmond affair "a political mess." He did not make clear whether he blamed the Chinese or the Americans for the mess.

"I have developed a slight twitch on my left side and above my left eye," Redmond wrote home early in 1962. "It is being treated now and I am hopeful it will go away. I guess it is another sign that I am getting old."

More than that, it was simply another sign that Redmond, who had now spent more than ten years in Chinese prisons, was no closer to release than he had been from the first day he was captured. His body was physically breaking down from the poor conditions he lived under. The Chinese no longer bothered to interrogate him. They, like most American officials, had simply chosen to forget about him.

"The CIA still cared," said Sol Friedman, now handling more and more of the family business. "They continued to send money so that we could continue to pursue the case. They clipped articles and sent me every reference to American prisoners they found in the world press. They stayed in close touch with the situation, but they couldn't seem to do much of anything to help move things along."

In the fall of 1962 Mrs. Redmond embarked on another journey to Shanghai to visit Hugh in prison.

"She had great hopes that something might happen this time," said Ruth Boyle. "She simply couldn't stop believing they would let him go. She also wanted badly to see him again."

In October of 1963, she took off once again on the torturous journey to China. It was to be the last time she would see her son.

I was able to visit Hugh four times, she wrote in 1963. *I was first told that I could only see him two times since my visa would expire. I protested that it was not my fault that I was delayed a day in Hong Kong and had to take a train instead of a plane. As a result of my protest, I received an extension so that I could visit Hugh four times. They would not allow me to stay an additional day so that I could see him on his birthday.*

Prior to visiting Hugh at the prison, I was again advised that the same eleven rules were in existence, and that I could only speak to him about our family in Yonkers, friends and non political events that had taken place in the United States.

Hugh appeared to be in good health, and the twitch that was evident on the side of his face during my last visit was gone. His mind appeared keen, but he seemed to have a vacant look in his eyes. He indicated that he had visited the infirmary twice, but could not tell me the reason. His clothes seemed to be falling off him, and I requested permission to purchase him a heavy padded coat and pants. I had brought with me heavy socks, underwear and three pair of shoes. When I gave the guards the shoes, they laughed and said he really needed them since they had clocked him walking fifteen miles or more a day. Hugh said when he had no books to read he used to pace up and down in his cell. Also, he was allowed out now into the prison yard for half an hour a day. I had also brought with me two suitcases crammed with food and clothing for Hugh.

I was able to leave money with him; therefore he would be able to purchase things through the guards from time to time. I was able to have dinner brought into the prison and eat with him. As usual the interpreter and two prison guards sat with us at the table all the time that I talked with Hugh.

Hugh seemed cheerful enough and was concerned about my health on this long journey. He indicated that he had one dream. That was to take the long journey home.

Mrs. Redmond returned to her Yonkers home after the trip. Once again she was interviewed extensively and appeared at several functions held by local organizations interested in helping Redmond get out of China.

"The trips were all very grueling for her," says Ruth Boyle. "What sustained her was the thought that something would happen, that the Chinese might relent, that suddenly she would receive a phone call from a Chinese official saying Hugh could leave with her."

It did not happen. There was always a period of long silence after she returned home. The letters from Hugh which seemed to arrive regularly toward the middle of the month always slowed down after she came back home. It was as if the Chinese wanted to read what Mrs. Redmond was saying to the press and in public before they would allow the normal flow of mail to resume.

Through 1964 and 1965 the letters came regularly, one a month, usually hand written all on one side of lined paper, sometimes spilling over to the other side if there were a major family event to comment on, a birth, the death of an elderly relative, an illness, an accomplishment by one of his nieces or nephews. The tone was generally straightforward and pleasant. Letters written around Christmas time were usually the cheeriest.

On December 4, 1965, Hugh wrote:

Dear Mother,

Merry Christmas to you and to the Boyles. And a Happy New Year to all, too. I suppose you will all spend the day together at Ruthie's place. I hope the children will find what they are wishing for under the tree. I hope there will be a little something there from me under the tree, too....

There was an article in the Chinese paper last month about a power failure that affected the northeast states including New York. What was the reason for such a large scale failure?

I am quite well and still plugging away at Chinese. Today I bought a Chinese book, not very difficult to read, that will keep me busy for two weeks. The newspaper doesn't present much difficulty now for me, ordinary articles I can read even without the dictionary. The big books and novels present a little more work and I look up about a word a page on the average.

Again Merry Christmas to one and all. I have nothing to send except my best wishes and the hope that we will all be together again one of these Christmas days.

As ever,

Hughie

P.S. Don't forget to stuff little Ruthie and the others with ice cream when they visit you."

In the early days of 1966 small stories began appearing in the world press about turmoil in China. Most of these stories originated with foreign diplomats who had been in China. The Chinese government suppressed all information about unrest. The crops had failed. There were severe food shortages. Conditions continued to worsen. Dramatic changes in the Chinese government were being reported through sources in Hong Kong. All observers agreed that conditions inside China were becoming more difficult and the government was become more oppressive. Fear was every where. Soon there were reports from inside the country that bands of hard-line Communists, young fanatics, mostly students, marauding night riders and terrorists known as Red Guards had spread violence, terror and destruction throughout China. The Red Guards, fanatic warriors devoted to Mao, attacked any public sign of opposition to his thoughts, deeds and influence and thought nothing of killing those persons suspected of any form of disagreement with Chairman Mao. They seemed especially hostile, as had been the case in the earliest days of the Communist takeover in Shanghai, toward foreigners.

Hugh Redmond's letters no longer arrived regularly. Instead of one letter a month, as before, they came once every second month. When they did arrive there were strange phrasings in them. He addressed his letters "Dear Mom." He had never addressed any letter to her in any way other than "Dear Mother" until now.

"He never called her anything but 'Mother,' " says Ruth Boyle. "He simply never used the term 'Mom' at all in any context."

His writing, always clear, clean and legible, became narrower, more difficult to read, with words crossed out, phrases scribbled, and odd spacing.

"It simply wasn't Hugh writing any more," said Ruth. "It just wasn't."

Instead of the once a month ritual, the letters fell from once every other month in 1966 to only two in the first half of 1967. The tone of the letters changed as well. Hugh would always write after receiving a package, "Thank you for the October package. I especially liked the candies." One letter in 1967 included the following: "Why did you send me canned meat again? I told you a dozen times I didn't want it any more. Also don't send any more of that terrible coffee. I don't need it."

Mrs. Redmond, attuned to every nuance in his letters, each change in his handwriting, every structural change, grew terribly concerned. She sensed, as a mother would, that Hugh was not himself. Either these letters were being written for him and were complete forgeries or he had been damaged now beyond repair by all the years of torturous treatment.

Then one day in 1967 Mrs. Redmond collapsed.

She had suffered a severe stroke. She was rushed to a hospital and given emergency treatment. Although she began to make a recovery, she would never be truly well again. She regained some of her speech and could walk unaided for a while. Now seventy years of age, she would never regain all her faculties.

Ruth Redmond was as much a victim of the Chinese torture tactics as was her son.

Ruth Boyle took over most of the letter writing chores after her mother became ill. Mrs. Redmond could scratch out her name or write a line, but the rest of the letter writing job was taken over by Hugh's sister. When Redmond learned of his mother's stroke, he wrote a sympathetic letter home.

In early August of 1967 a new letter arrived from Hugh. It was dated July 4th, 1967. It again had the familiar greeting, "Dear Mother," but the script seemed more like that of Hugh's than any other letter in the past eighteen months. It began:

> *It just dawned on me as I wrote the date above that today is the Fourth of July. Did you have a big celebration in the park with fireworks and all? I remember how much fun it was when we were kids and you would take me and Ruthie down to the park on the Fourth of July and she would cover her ears as the firecrackers exploded and I would leap for joy at the excitement of it all. I can still remember the first time I had my own firecrackers to explode on the lot across from the house. What a splendid day.*

There were a few more references to family matters, including a question about an anchor fence that had been put in at Ruth Boyle's home, a reference to goods sent him in a recent package and the mention of several books he liked. Then he wrote,

>*Don't forget to buy ice cream for the children. My best*
>*regards to you all.*

Love,

Hugh

P.S. Please send me a bottle of aspirin.

Those were the last written words ever seen from Hugh Francis Redmond.

No letter came in August after that. Or September. Or October. Even the ritualistic Christmas letter in November or December was missing. Mrs. Redmond, recovering her strength, asked Sol Friedman to explore the matter. Friedman discussed it with the CIA.

"They told me they had no way of getting information from inside China. They had been cut off from their sources there. China was a terrible problem for them, a country so huge and important, and yet with so little information available," Friedman said.

Friedman wrote to every ambassador around the world with diplomatic relations with China. Some actually were afraid to help. Many feared repercussions from the Chinese. Friedman visited embassies in Europe, talked with Chinese officials, left messages with clerks, got audiences with ambassadors abroad. Even with those countries which seemed willing to help, no further information was ever received.

Then came an idea put forth by the CIA.

"One afternoon a couple of agents came into my office and said we might try a tactic they had used successfully in other cases," Friedman recalls. "They told me it might be possible to buy information."

Friedman called a press conference. He announced that a fund would be started with the express purpose of raising one million dollars to be used to buy information concerning the condition and future of Hugh Redmond. The million dollar fund was advertised heavily. Money was given to Friedman by the CIA to help publicize it. The Agency seemed serious about its attempts to aid the cause.

"People made contributions," Friedman said. "We got donations from all sorts of groups and individuals. But it didn't amount to much. We couldn't get anywhere near a million dollars. It was impossible. What money we collected was donated to various charities."

"I sat in hotel rooms all over Europe waiting for information that was supposed to be coming. I read letters from people who had been in China. I talked to people who had known Redmond in Shanghai. I also read letters from opportunists who would make up nonsensical information in hopes of landing that million dollar reward. It was all terribly difficult, aggravating and frustrating," Friedman said.

During those early days of 1970, as Friedman waited, hoping for some useful information about Redmond, four names were linked together in the American press whenever the question of prisoners in China was discussed. There was Redmond, alleged businessman, convicted by the Chinese as a spy, now serving his nineteenth year of a life sentence for espionage. The second man was John Thomas Downey, alleged civilian passenger on a routine flight over China, convicted as a spy by the Chinese, now serving his eighteenth year of a life sentence. The third man, Richard George Fecteau, was also an alleged civilian passenger on the same flight as Downey, now serving his eighteenth year of a twenty year term after being convicted of espionage. The fourth man was Bishop James E. Walsh of the Maryknoll order in Maryknoll, New York, arrested in 1958 by the Chinese after more than a half century in China as a missionary, tried and convicted in 1960 and sentenced to twenty years.

Maryknoll, a training ground for missionaries, is a pleasant drive along the Hudson River, north of New York City. From afar a Chinese style pagoda roof stands out over the pleasantly landscaped areas among a collection of simple stone buildings. Maryknoll was founded as a Catholic mission in 1904. Bishop Walsh was among four young priests of this Catholic order who would carry the word of God to Shanghai, China in 1918. The young priest remained there through 1936, returned to Maryknoll, and then continued his work in China in 1948.

It is here, among the quiet of rustling trees, and the singing of birds that Bishop James E. Walsh returned after his release from prison. In his eighty sixth year, confined by ill health to his quarters at Maryknoll, after a lifetime of service to God and his people, Bishop James E. Walsh was living out his final days.

Bishop Walsh could not see me when I visited Maryknoll but he did write afterwards.

> *It would be a waste of time for you to visit me here at Maryknoll in hopes of obtaining information about Hugh Redmond since I have none to give. I did not know Mr. Redmond and I never saw him in prison or elsewhere at any time. In fact, I never saw any foreigner at any time during my twelve years of confinement in the Nan T'an House of Confinement and in Ward Road Prison.*

> *Actually I had heard of Mr. Redmond when he was first arrested. The fact was reported in the local English language newspaper at the time. But I only recall the circumstances that several foreigners commented on the occasion that Mr. Redmond was a respectable businessman whereas the several other men arrested at the same time were questionable characters. Apart from that I never heard a word about Mr. Redmond at any time.*

Bishop Walsh denied at the time of his arrest in 1958 that he had any contact with or served any function for the United States government. It was made clear several years later in investigations of CIA methods that the use of missionaries as suppliers of information was a common practice in the CIA. There was no way of knowing if Bishop Walsh was, indeed, a conduit of information or had any contacts with the CIA.

From the time of his arrest in 1958, Bishop Walsh was often linked in stories with Downey and Fecteau, confessed CIA agents and with Hugh Redmond, the hard-nosed non confessor.

In the early afternoon of July 10, 1970 the telephone rang in Maryknoll's offices in Hong Kong, Stanley House. The call was for Father J. G. Sullivan, young regional superior of the Hong Kong province, from the American consulate in Hong Kong, the China desk.

"Bishop Walsh is at Lu Wo. What do you want done with him?

That was the first word that the world was to hear that Bishop Walsh had been set free by the Communist Chinese at the bridge crossing point between Communist China and the British Crown Colony. An ambulance was quickly dispatched to the crossing point and the elderly priest was seated in a wheelchair, escorted to the ambulance and then on to a hospital for examination. He seemed in relatively good shape considering his age and his years of confinement.

"I am very happy to be free once again," he told reporters in a hastily summoned press conference. "I never thought I would ever see the day of my release. I felt I would not live long enough to complete my sentence of twenty years and would die in prison. It has been hard for me to believe, even now, that I have been released. I have no bitterness toward those who tried and condemned me. I could never feel any anger with any Chinese. I felt that way almost from the first day I set foot in China in 1918, and my feelings have grown stronger with the years, even during my imprisonment."

"Would you go back to China if you had an opportunity?" he was asked.

"Oh, yes, surely," he said. "I spent half my life in China and I suppose that makes me half Chinese at least. I feel that it is my country, to a large extent."

Bishop Walsh said he had no advance knowledge that he was to be released. He had been told to pack his bags at 8 A.M. two days earlier. A doctor came by to check his condition. By 10 A.M. on the morning of July 8th, he was aboard a train bound for Canton, accompanied by a doctor, two interpreters, a photographer and three policemen. The doctor had taken his pulse every hour. The train was air conditioned. He stayed overnight in Canton and then continued on by train to Hong Kong. He was processed at the crossing point and ordered to walk across the border alone. It was 2 P.M., July 19th, 1970.

One hour later the Hsinhua News Agency made the announcement in Chinese language broadcasts throughout the country and in an English language broadcast in Peking. The news agency announced that the American priest and spy, Bishop James E. Walsh, had been released for humanitarian reasons after serving twelve years.

Bishop Walsh had made a complete confession of his crimes. This announcement accompanied the release of every foreigner since the Communists took over the country in 1949. The Hsinhua News Agency coupled the news of Bishop Walsh's release with one other announcement.

Hugh Francis Redmond was dead.

Chapter 18

Ashes to Ashes

The long days and nights between July 4, 1967 and July 19, 1970 were filled with anguish for Yonkers attorney Sol Friedman. He had immersed himself almost totally in the Hugh Redmond case.

With CIA money, he traveled across America and into more than a dozen countries abroad seeking information on Redmond after his final letter came. He talked with hundreds of people, many of whom had been in Ward Prison in Shanghai, or in other Chinese prisons. He waited in hotel rooms for phone calls that never came. He answered phone calls from crackpots. intent only on amusing themselves with false information about the case. He wrote over a thousand letters to Chinese leaders seeking information on Redmond. He wrote to American officials, to foreigners who had entered and left China sometime during that three year period. He contacted newsmen and all available sources inside China. He spoke to religious leaders, civic leaders, representatives of numerous organizations he thought might be able to help. After Mrs. Redmond suffered a second and more severe stroke in 1969, Friedman, using Redmond funds at his disposal, assumed most of the financial burden of caring for her. She was placed in a nursing home at the end of that year. Finally, because of her illness, she was freed of any anxiety about her son.

"Those three years," says Ruth Boyle, "were probably the worst. My mother was no longer able to understand but I waited by the phone each day for some word from Sol. Even if Hughie was dead, as long as we knew, as long as it was final, that would have been easier to take than this terrible emptiness."

In early April of 1970, Friedman received a note from a pacifist named Earle Reynolds who had sailed into Chinese waters. Reynolds had been arrested and detained. He was held, questioned and finally released without charges. After his release he was contacted by Friedman. Reynolds said he had heard Redmond's name mentioned while he was held by the Chinese, and that he was told that Redmond was alive. That was all he knew.

For three years now there had been no communication from Hugh. Why had the Chinese finally cut him off? What had the Red Guards done to him? What tortures of mind and body might he now be subjected to? Why was he being deprived of contact with his family so that they did not know whether he was dead or alive? What did Hugh Redmond represent to the Chinese? Had this brave man become an intolerable burden to his captors?

Friedman slept fitfully in the early morning hours of July 10, 1970. His case load was heavy and his office desk was filled with unfinished work. The Redmond case and other charity work were taking more and more of his time. He looked forward to a much needed vacation. Perhaps, he thought, a couple of weeks away with his wife, Leah, and he could regain his perspective. Maybe then he could come up with some new methods for attacking the Redmond case, some new roads to explore, some new leads to pursue. Mrs. Redmond was no longer competent but Sol Friedman felt more motivated than ever to carry on the quest for Redmond's release.

The ringing of the phone early in the morning hours of that July 10th shocked him awake. He reached for the light switch and turned a small table lamp on. He caught the phone after the third ring.

"Hello."

"Is this Sol Friedman?"

"Yes it is. Who is this?"

"This is the Associated Press calling. Do you know that Hugh Redmond is dead?"

Friedman jerked up in bed, his nerve endings suddenly jangled, his heart pumping faster, his hands starting to sweat as he held the phone.

"Dead? What do you mean? How do you know?"

"It was announced by the Chinese news agency, picked up by Reuters and transmitted to us. Hugh Redmond committed suicide in April. They broke the news about Redmond with the announcement about freeing Bishop Walsh."

"That's impossible," Friedman said. "It doesn't make any sense. Why would he commit suicide after all these years?"

Friedman discussed the case for a few more minutes with the reporter for the Associated Press, hung up and turned to his wife, who was at his side, listening sympathetically to his side of the conversation.

"Hugh Redmond is dead," he told her. "The Chinese say he committed suicide."

"Oh, God, Sol," Mrs. Friedman said. Then she broke down and began to sob.

"At least," Friedman said, "Ruth will never have to know."

In minutes the phone at the Friedman home was ringing again, with newspapers calling for comment, the wire services calling for further information, radio and television stations asking for interviews and appointments being set to discuss the bizarre ending of this strange case.

Now, years later, Friedman still has difficulty discussing the events of that morning.

"Why? That's what I keep asking myself. Why would he kill himself? Did he really kill himself or did they murder him? Why did they hold back the news for three months? Why did they wait until they freed Bishop Walsh to announce it? Why was Hugh Redmond alone held until his death, and Bishop Walsh, John Downey and Richard Fecteau all allowed to leave? It simply had to be because Hugh fought them, because he wouldn't talk. That made him different. That separated his case from that of any other spy they ever had," Friedman said.

The Chinese news agency gave out the news about Redmond's death in a terse addendum to the announcement of the release of Bishop Walsh. They said that on the late afternoon of April 13, 1970, Redmond had secreted a razor blade, sent to him from home in one of his parcels, in his cell. He had used the razor blade when guards left him alone for the evening meal, cutting the artery of the medial aspect of his left elbow. He had then, they said, slashed the blade across his left wrist, switched the blade to the bloody left hand and cut a deep gash in his right wrist. Some minutes later, the Chinese said, he was discovered mortally wounded, lying face down on the floor of his cell. He was quickly carried to the prison infirmary, blood covering most of his body and clothes, his eyes shut, his face a chalky white. The Chinese said emergency treatment was rendered Redmond immediately. It was to no avail. At 6:03 P.M. on April 13, 1970, he was reported to have expired.

"The body has already been cremated," said the Chinese news report, "and the culprit Redmond's death has been reported to the Red Cross Society in China and they in turn have relayed the information to the American Red Cross for passage to his relatives."

In an interview Sol Friedman told a reporter that day, "I just don't buy it. I don't believe the story. The release of Bishop Walsh was announced at the same time as Hugh Redmond's death as a cover-up for this evil deed. This is an example of the worst kind of man's inhumanity to man."

The Chinese news agency had always described Redmond as that "notorious spy." Now in a late evening broadcast they described him that day with these words: "He was a United States imperialist spy who had been dispatched to China by the Office of Strategic Services, predecessor of the hated Central Intelligence Agency, who had carried out espionage against the Chinese people in Shanghai, Peking and Shenyang and thus committed grave crimes."

Friedman said after the notification that the matter would not be dropped.

"We will make inquiries to the United States State Department and to the International Red Cross for more information on this case. We will attempt to bring it before the United Nations and the conscience of all mankind," Friedman said.

He did not pursue it. The reason was simple. He wanted the remains of Hugh Redmond shipped back from China for burial in Yonkers. The Chinese would certainly not cooperate on this delicate matter if there was public embarrassment or undue harassment on the issue.

An hour after Redmond's death was announced on the news service wires, there was a knock on the door of Ruth Boyle's home. The sun was not yet up as Bernard Boyle moved cautiously to his front door. He peered out from behind a window shade.

"Who is it?"

"Is this the Boyle residence? We're from the *Daily News*. We would like a picture of Mrs. Boyle to go with the story of her brother's death. Hugh Redmond, the Chinese spy."

Ruth Boyle shook her head as she described how she found out about her brother's death.

"It was so cruel," she says. "They came around at that ungodly hour, woke us up, told us this horrible news. Such coldness. I couldn't believe people could be that way."

The reporter and photographer from the *Daily News* were finally allowed in the house after much pleading. They talked to the Boyles and a picture was taken showing Ruth Boyle holding an old picture of her brother. They never showed any compassion for her situation. Ruth Boyle remembers them as vultures.

As the news of Redmond's death spread, letters of condolence and sympathy began arriving from across the country and around the world at the Boyle home. Thousands of cards and letters, enough to fill several cartons, arrived from strangers who had been touched by this drama of human dignity and courage.

Reverend Joseph McCormack, ill and aging (he was to die three years later), wrote a long handwritten letter to Ruth Boyle.

> *Hugh was not the kind of man to give up,* Father McCormack wrote Redmond's sister. *He never did commit suicide. He was too brave and true and honorable for that. He was murdered. Don't ask me how I know. I just do. He was generous in every way and loved to divide the contents of the boxes he received from your mother with all of us. He never used a rough word. He was always polite and good company. He attended his Catholic*

duties and assisted me at secret masses whenever we could say one. Considering his fine work during the war in Europe and his long suffering days in China, I would consider him deserving of some special honor in the USA. I hope he receives a medal or memorial of some kind.

Perhaps the most telling letter came from Jean Pasqualini (Bao Ruowang) in Paris. This man of Chinese/French parentage, who had undergone so much suffering at the hands of the Communists before his release in 1964, knew how they thought and acted. He had tried to obtain information about Hugh Redmond from inside China ever since Sol Friedman first contacted him in 1967.

It was with mixed feelings of shock, anger and horror that I learned of the news that Hugh Redmond 'committed suicide' on April 13, he wrote to Friedman.

The Chinese Communist authorities in their laconic announcement added that Redmond slashed his wrists with a razor blade and he died from loss of blood.

Immediately after reading this awful bit of news on the wires, I telephoned Mr. Rousset, whom you met during your stopover in Paris. Both of us find the explanation of the death of Hugh Redmond as being totally unacceptable, and that the Chinese Communist authorities have enmeshed themselves in a net of lies and contradictory statements.

People under confinement in China, even those enjoying a privileged status, are strictly forbidden to have in their possession objects made of metal. The sole exception is made for enamelware needed for washing and eating purposes. Prisoners are given a haircut and a shave by the prison barber at regular intervals. For cases deemed 'dangerous,' 'unreliable,' or 'weak-minded,' their beards are clipped with a clipper. How did Redmond come into possession of a razor blade?

Assuming that Redmond did succeed in getting hold of a razor blade with which he managed to slash his wrists, how could he lose blood in big amounts when the guard was supposed to look into his cell regularly and at very short intervals? Reports that Redmond was sick would place him in the prison hospital. There the surveillance is even more strict. How could he have bled to death under the ever-watchful eye of the prison personnel?

The Chinese Communists can not evade responsibility for Redmond's death. Suicide even puts them in a more compromising position. Either they drove him to it, or they caused his death by not giving him the attention to which, as a prisoner, he is entitled at all hours of the day.

Please convey my condolences to Mrs. Redmond.

P.S. Here's a more cheerful note. If Redmond did really commit suicide (I say IF), then I wouldn't want to be either the warden on duty of the block he was confined in, or even the director of the prison. They would have had a lot of explanations to make. Not to us, but to their superiors.

Friedman communicated with the American Red Cross. He requested that the remains of Hugh Francis Redmond be shipped home as the Chinese indicated they were willing to do. The American Red Cross immediately contacted the Red Cross Society of China and discussed details of the arrangements.

There was no peace for Sol Friedman, who was haunted by the way in which they had received the final news about Redmond. There was no way to prove what had really happened. He refused to accept the story of the suicide and agonized over his, and the CIA's inability to get at the truth. There would never be any further word from the Chinese on the matter.

As Friedman awaited the arrival of Redmond's remains, another news clipping arrived in the mail from his CIA contact. It was a small item from a British newspaper. It detailed the release in early August, 1970 of a British engineer named George Watt. He had been held for three years in several prisons and had finally been released — as always — after signing a detailed confession of his alleged crimes.

"I was questioned and treated miserably until I decided to confess to whatever they asked me," Watt said. "After I signed the confession I was moved from one prison to another. My room was larger in the second prison. I was fed better, I was questioned hardly at all and I was finally released unharmed."

Watt recalled the first prison he was in as a horrendous place with meager rations of food, terrible treatment, horrendous conditions. Life there had been a torturous experience.

"I was only there a few months," he said, "and then I was removed to a better prison."

Before he was moved from this torturous place, Ward Road Prison in Shanghai, he remembered one night in particular. He was in his cell, down the hall from a corridor from which he heard some ghastly sounds.

"It was an American voice. I could tell," he said. "He was screaming in pain, as if he was being brutally beaten. I could hardly make out the words. He was shouting, 'Don't close the door, don't close the door, don't close me in here.' It sounded to me as if the man was insane."

There was no way of knowing who that voice belonged to, but it would be a fair guess that George Watt had heard the voice of Hugh Redmond in his final hours of agony.

After Redmond's death was reported, the CIA contacted Friedman. A representative showed up at his Yonkers office with papers for Friedman to sign. The man from the CIA said the government would begin processing all the papers necessary to wind up the Redmond affair. They said his back pay, allowances and benefits would come to a substantial amount of money. The final total was $161,513.49. A check for that amount was dispatched to Friedman. He put it all in a trust fund for Mrs. Redmond's last days, after which it was to go to Mrs. Boyle and the

Boyle children.

There would be money for ice cream from Uncle Hughie for many years to come.

Chapter **19**

The Final Chapter

The funeral cortege moved slowly down South Broadway in Yonkers from the Flynn Memorial Home to the Church of St. John the Baptist. It was a blistering hot morning, August 3, 1970 and guests waited fitfully at the church. Every seat in the old church was filled, a few with Redmond relatives, a few with steadfast friends from the past like Bernie Connolly who was seated in a back row. Most were strangers, politicians who wanted to be in on a major Yonkers event, newsmen assigned to come up with a tear-jerking story, television cameramen and sound men determined to create sixty seconds of terse film. There was a carnival atmosphere at the church, old politicians greeting each other, the newsmen shouting at each other across the aisle, curious townsfolk, some in shorts and summer shirts, some with tousled kids in tow, very few interested in reflecting on the life and death of Hugh Redmond.

A missa cantata Mass was celebrated. Ruth Boyle accepted condolences on behalf of the family. The politicians in town squeezed her hand in greeting, looking pointedly at the television cameras rather than at Ruth Boyle. Within thirty minutes, the sweltering church stood silent.

A procession formed outside the church for a parade to Oakland Cemetery. An honor escort of some thirty Yonkers policemen at the head of the cortege, brass buttons and belt buckles glittering in the summer sun, were followed by the representatives of the local American Legion Post, including some Legionnaires who had fought in France in World War I.

Then came the sleek black limousine of the Flynn Memorial Home.

A handsome young attendant drove the limousine and an assistant sat at his side. In the rear of the car lay what were purported to be the remains of Hugh Francis Redmond. An American flag covered the casket.

A troop of Boy Scouts followed behind the limousine. Then came other uniformed groups — firemen, VFW, Sea Scouts, a Little League team, a row of National Guard soldiers with a drum and bugle corps bringing up the rear.

They marched slowly past the stores and factories of South Broadway, past the nursing home where Ruth Redmond sat in quiet serenity, past the lines of curious, across a major intersection and finally into the gates of the old cemetery grounds.

The limousine carrying the remains of Hugh Redmond and all the cars that followed the walking procession now parked just inside the iron gates. They began making their slow and careful walk to the gravesite. The procession walked along the old foot path, across a small intersection of cemetery paths. A heavy silence descended on them, and only the scuffing of shoes against the cobblestones of the foot path could be heard. The heat seemed to rise out of the earth on this sweltering and steamy day. Now the narrow path rose along a small hill, leading to the family plot. The police escort reached the Redmond plot and gathered around the freshly dug grave.

Three young Boy Scout drummers, on a signal from the cemetery attendant, took deep breaths, held their sticks high and began a slow, emotional drum roll. Ba...rooom. Ba...rooom. Ba...rooom. They struck their drums lightly, in unison, sending the sound of the drum rolls soaring up and over the group that had assembled at the grave site.

Sol Friedman moved closer to the open grave. He held a piece of paper in his hand. The drum rolls continued. Ba...rooom Ba...rooom Ba...rooom. Now the Scouts were signaled and the drum rolls came to a halt. The casket was lifted from its mooring, placed on waiting straps and lowered slowly into the grave.

A fourth Boy Scout, standing alone high above the site on a hill overlooking the grave, put a bugle to his lips. He stretched the first long notes of Taps, his lips pursing hard against the mouthpiece, his cheeks filled with air, his eyes closed, his mind concentrating on delivering a perfect rendering, his heart set on performing his very best. He played magnificently, and now he was finished. He brought the bugle down to his hip, turned slowly and walked down the opposite side of the hill.

At the grave Sol Friedman nodded toward the remains of Hugh Redmond, a man he had never met and was now called on to eulogize. He ran a handkerchief across his sweating face and put on his glasses. Then he began speaking in a firm, controlled voice.

> *Today we bury the ashes of Hugh Francis Redmond. Certainly no one can bury the indomitable spirit and courage of this man. He suffered the indignity of his imprisonment as only the bravest of men could endure. Never once could the Chinese government exact a confession or an admission of guilt from him. How easy it would have been to make a spurious confession. Thus today we honor and consecrate in this solemn moment of remembrance the spirit of this brave human being whose love for his mother and father and sister, and in turn their unending devotion and love for him, gave him the courage and fortitude to suffer his nineteen long years of confinement and the heavy, heavy silence of those last three years since July 4, 1967. Hugh is now at rest. May we all learn from this tragedy once again the utter stupidity of man's inhumanity to man.*

Friedman stepped back from the grave. He closed his eyes and prayed silently. There were some final words, a prayer from the priest, and now the first shovelful of earth was thrown into the grave. The group moved away, began winding their way back along the path from which they had come as cemetery workmen quickly went about their task.

Sol Friedman returned to his office later that afternoon, signed some government papers and the processing of all rights and benefits to the Redmond estate was completed.

Early in March of 1973, Ruth Redmond, now seventy three, died quietly at the Yonkers nursing home. She was buried alongside her son and husband in the Oakland Cemetery, her death almost unnoticed in the local press.

In her upstate New York home, Ruth Boyle dug out some old letters, photographs and mementoes of her brother. She laughed as she pulled out some baby pictures of Hugh to show a visitor.

"You know," she said, "I never knew Hugh as anything but a young man. I'm a grandmother now and when I think of him, I can remember him best as a kid. He would be nearly seventy years old now, but I can still only think of him as a boy with wavy hair, with a little smile and a mischievous face."

She reached down into a box and pulled out a letter. She examined the date on the front and began to read slowly to herself. Then she handed it to her visitor.

> *Dear Ruthie,*
>
> *It is with much joy that I have learned that you are now a grandmother. My God, where have all the years gone? It is so hard for me to believe the news about you. It seems only yesterday that we wrestled at home and you played football with us and I treated you badly like a big brother usually does. I want to say now that it was only out of love. I hope you will accept my apology. I know I should have said these things years ago. Better late than never.*
>
> *It is warming up pleasantly now after a cold winter and the air seems so fresh again with the new season. I want so much to be with you and smell the trees and watch the seasons turn. I am filled with hope that this glorious day will come for us soon.*

Ruth Boyle watched as the visitor read the letter. Then she shook her head, bit her lip as her eyes filled with tears, and left the room. There were sobs coming from a back room as her visitor self-consciously left the house, almost ashamed to be walking free in the crisp afternoon air.

✳

There seems no reason for the death of Hugh Francis Redmond. He could have acquiesced like all the others, he could have signed a piece of paper, and escaped with his life. It is all so terribly cruel, so pointless, so unrewarding in the deepest sense. Yet he was brave, he was special, he was a man with great strength of character and integrity. Patriotism ran deep in him. His friends and relatives knew and understood.

The trees were a beautiful golden color now as early fall tinged the edges of the maples in deep burnt orange. In a small park along the Hudson River Valley two husky youngsters, one wearing a football jersey, the other a sweatsuit, heaved long football passes to each other, shouting and diving for the ball as they had seen on so many fall Saturday afternoons on their television sets. A man walked toward them. They continued to throw passes. Then a ball bounced away from one of them and landed at the man's feet. He bent down, picked up the ball and threw a perfect spiral to the closest youngster.

"Do you fellows play here often?" he asked.

"Oh, sure," the boy in the football jersey said. "I just live across the street and Donny here lives down the block."

"Do you know the name of this park? Do you know who it's named after?"

"Yeah. Redmond Park," he said. "For Hugh Redmond, everybody in Yonkers knows him. He's the guy who fought in the war against the Chinese."

Bleachers surrounded the field. The man sat there, watching the boys have their catch for a while. The day was turning colder and darker. The man left. The boys never noticed.

The End

Author's Note: Most of the interviews for this book were conducted in the early 1980's.